READY

START

SCHOOL!

Nurturing and Guiding Your Child Through Preschool & Kindergarten

SANDRA F. RIEF, M.A.

Library of Congress Cataloging-in-Publication Data

Rief, Sandra F.
    Ready—start—school! : nurturing and guiding your child through preschool
and kindergarten / Sandra F. Rief.
        p. cm.
    Includes index.
    ISBN 0-7352-0299-0 (pbk.)
        1. Education, Preschool—Parent participation.   2. Kindergarten.   3. Child
development.   4. Learning, Psychology of.   I. Title.

LB1140.35.P37 R54 2001
372.21—dc21   2001033922

Printed in the United States of America

10 9 8 7 6 5 4 3 2 1

ISBN 0-7352-0299-0

 **Paramus, NJ 07652**

http://www.phdirect.com

*This book is dedicated to all of our children
with love and hope that they all grow up healthy,
happy, and successful in school and in life.*

ABOUT THE AUTHOR

Sandra F. Rief (B.A., M.A., University of Illinois) is an award-winning educator with over 20 years of experience teaching in public schools. She is a nationally and internationally recognized speaker, consultant, and teacher-trainer specializing in academic, behavioral, and instructional strategies for meeting the needs of children with learning, attention, and behavioral challenges.

She is the author of several books, including *How to Reach and Teach ADD/ADHD Children* (The Center for Applied Research in Education, 1993), *How to Reach and Teach All Students in the Inclusive Classroom* (co-authored with Julie Heimburge, The Center for Applied Research in Education, 1996), *The ADD/ADHD Checklist: An Easy Reference for Parents & Teachers* (Prentice Hall, 1998), and *Alphabet Learning Center Activities Kit* (co-authored with Nancy Fetzer, The Center for Applied Research in Education, 2000). Sandra developed and presented a number of videos with Educational Resource Specialists, including *How to Help Your Child Succeed in School* (1997) and *Successful Classrooms: Effective Teaching Strategies for Raising Achievement in Reading and Writing* (with Linda Fisher and Nancy Fetzer, 1999).

ACKNOWLEDGMENTS

I wish to thank and acknowledge the following:

My own family:

Itzik, for being such a loving, supportive husband, and exceptional father to our children

Gil, Jackie, and Ariel, our incredibly wonderful children who give us such pride and joy; Benjamin, our precious son and baby brother, who will *always* be in our hearts

My parents, the greatest, dearest, and most positive role models in my life

The many, many friends, family members, teachers and other educators, parents and grandparents of students, and others I have admired, been influenced by, and learned from as both a parent and a teacher

Levana Estline, Julia Croom, Christina Evans, Sue Sward, Judy Medoff, Rachell Clavell, Betsy Arnold, Marcia Giafaglione, and Yael Estline, the highly respected, outstanding group of preschool and kindergarten teachers and preschool director, who let me interview them, and share their wisdom and insights in the section *What the Experts Say*

Lorraine Lubliner, who inspired me when I was a child to want to spend my life as she did—dedicated to teaching and helping those children with learning difficulties and behavioral challenges who find it such a struggle to succeed in school

My most wonderful editor, Susan Kolwicz, and publisher, Win Huppuch, at Prentice Hall, for the pleasure and privilege of working with you over the years, and for having asked me to author this book and the others in the series

INTRODUCTION

There is no greater gift than our children, and no greater responsibility than parenthood. We all learn how to parent through on-the-job training. Those of us who have raised more than one child know that we are different parents to each of our children, as we learn from experience. What may have put us into a state of panic with our first child is a familiar event with our second or third child. With each of our children being so different from one another in personality, temperament, developmental abilities, strengths, and weaknesses, we learn to be flexible and adapt, treating each child differently, according to his or her needs.

This book will validate much of what you are already doing with your child. Much of the content is common-sense parenting advice. However, some of the topics may be unfamiliar to you, especially if you are a first-time parent or if you haven't kept abreast of educational expectations and the latest research on child development. It is my hope that this book will serve as a resource and reference during the early childhood years and that you will find some useful information and strategies you wish to try with your child.

Don't feel you are an inadequate parent if you haven't been implementing many of the strategies in your home. No one is a perfect parent or able to do all of what is recommended—even with the best of efforts and intentions. Some of the suggestions or strategies are ones you will find worth trying. Do whatever you are able to do that makes sense and feels appropriate to you and your family. It is better to try only a few new things at a time rather than attempt to implement many changes all at once.

This book focuses on what parents can do to help their children of preschool or kindergarten age. The reference to "parents" includes all of those who are raising and parenting children—whatever the family configuration may be, or whoever is assuming responsibility for the child.

The message of this book is to *enjoy* your young child. Take the precious gift of early childhood and have fun with it, nurture it, *pay attention* to it. These are critical years that set the foundation for your child's current and future learning, growth, and development in every arena—social, emotional, behavioral, cognitive, self-confidence, attitude, physical/mental health, and so forth. Your attention, recognition, and approval mean everything to your child. Your child needs and thrives on your unconditional love, which is always there regardless of his or her performance, behavior, or abilities.

I am grateful and blessed to be a mother. My husband and I are fortunate to have raised three great kids, who managed to do well in school and are all currently in or have graduated from the colleges of their choice. We like to think that part of the credit for our children being the wonderful people they are is related to what we did as parents. In honesty, we must admit that our kids also turned out to be the terrific young adults they are *in spite* of what we did as parents. No matter how well intentioned and knowledgeable we are, we all make a lot of mistakes along the way as we parent—hopefully none so serious or irreparable that we cause harm to our children. Fortunately, children are resilient and adaptable. They are tolerant and forgiving of our flaws as parents.

The key—whatever our style of parenting—is that our children know the bottom line: that they are deeply loved and cared for. They need to know that, yes, there are other important things in their parents' lives (e.g., other people and relationships, work, hobbies, interests, community activities). However, they must know that nothing else is more important to their parents than *they* are, and they must feel that "My parents love me. My parents are interested in me and in what I think, feel, and do. My parents will take care of me. My parents will guide and teach me. My parents will put forth the energy and effort in their job of parenting me."

We now know that the years from age 3 to age 5 are critical. A great deal of brain development is taking place during this time. These are truly the formative years when the foundation for learning is established. There is much that you can do right now that will greatly enhance your child's chances for doing well in school (currently and in future years) and increase his or her ability to be successful in life. It is my hope that some of the information in this book will help you build that strong foundation and set a positive course for your child.

Best wishes,
Sandra Rief

CONTENTS

PART 3

Advice on Social, Behavioral,
and Discipline Issues

PART 4

Everything a Parent Needs to Know
on How Children Learn to Read

PART 5

Getting Your Child Organized and Ready for Writing, Math, and Homework

PART 6

What to Do if You Suspect Your Child Has a Developmental Delay or Disability

PART 7

What the Experts Say

THE CRITICAL ROLE OF PARENTS IN THEIR CHILD'S EDUCATION

Of all periods of your child's life, the years between the ages of 3 and 5—the preschool and kindergarten years—are crucial in your child's growth and development. These are also years when you, as parents, have a unique opportunity to influence how your child views the world and, most important, sees himself or herself as a learner. Through your loving, nurturing guidance and encouragement, your child naturally explores and experiments, perseveres and practices, takes risks and gains a feeling of mastery, competence, and success.

As your child's first and most important teacher and role model, you play an important role in helping your child acquire the foundational skills of all future learning: language and communication skills, motor skills (large and small muscle movements), social/emotional and behavioral skills, cognitive (thinking/reasoning) skills, and emergent-level literacy (reading/writing) skills.

Fortunately, parents don't need formal training to fulfill their role successfully as their child's primary teacher in these developmental skills. We teach our young children through our day-to-day interactions—when we talk with and play with them, when we cuddle up and read to them, and when we calmly and patiently help them to solve problems. Preschoolers and kindergartners gain massive amounts of new knowledge and competencies during these years as they lose their clumsiness and become stronger and more physically able to explore the world around them. Your child acquires language usage and vocabulary at an astonishing rate during the early childhood years. Children of this age are constantly wondering and questioning those around them, wanting to know why, why, why. They are eager and enthusiastic learners trying to understand themselves and their world, and gain independence and awareness. Given the opportunity, they will naturally absorb new information, make connections, and acquire most of the prerequisite skills for success in school.

Our children thrive from the interest, attention, and positive expectations we communicate to them. We shouldn't underestimate the impact of our role as models to our children. We are models when we show our children how we speak to others, treat others, work to improve ourselves and acquire new skills, tackle challenging situations, and use reading and writing daily for learning and for pleasure/entertainment. We need to remember that in spite of all our personal shortcomings, our children love us, want to please us, and aspire to be like us. As parents, that is an awesome privilege and responsibility!

PART 1

What Parents
Need to Know
About Their
3- to 5-Year-Olds

There is a difference in the rate children reach and acquire developmental milestones and skills in language, cognition/thinking, social/adaptive, behavior, sensory-motor, and academic readiness. One section of this book addresses developmental milestones of children and gives a rough estimate of what many children are able to do by their fourth, fifth, and sixth birthdays. It is helpful to know the kinds of pre-academic tasks and skills children need for school readiness—the prerequisites for learning how to read, write, and so forth. The section *What Schools Expect of Kindergartners by the End of the School Year* provides examples of performance standards or expectations of various school districts for students who are about to enter the first grade. Grade-level performance standards help teachers guide instruction. Although these standards vary across school districts, they should help you gain awareness of the concepts and skills children are generally taught during the kindergarten year.

Many parents of 5-year-olds or those soon to be turning 5 find themselves struggling with the decision of whether or not their child is ready to start kindergarten. The section *Enrolling Your Child in Kindergarten or Waiting Another Year* addresses this topic and offers suggestions for parents to consider when making an informed decision about what's right for their child.

All of the information in this part of the book is meant to serve as a reference in providing guidance and in helping you better gauge your young child's development. Of course, with any concerns or questions about your child's development or readiness, it is advised that you speak with your child's pediatrician, teacher, day-care provider, and other professionals.

Developmental Milestones
of 3- to 5-Year-Olds

Children learn and accomplish major developmental feats during the critical early childhood years. It is a time of wonder for parents as they watch their children grow by leaps and bounds each day. Keep your camera (and tape recorder) handy to record your child's growth during these precious growing years.

This section discusses developmental benchmarks or milestones for children from 3 to 5 years old. These milestones serve as a frame of reference for the skills/abilities children in this age group acquire in the areas of language, cognition/thinking, social/adaptive/behavioral (e.g., cooperation, following directions, getting along with and interacting with others, independence), and gross/fine motor (large and small muscle movement).

Children do not acquire skills at the same rate; there is a wide range of competencies among youngsters at different ages and grades. Development is frequently uneven in children. For example, your 3-year-old child may be able to perform all or most of the behaviors listed in this section involving motor skills but show some delays or immaturity in language skills. This is not uncommon, and in most cases it isn't cause to worry. If you do have any concerns, of course, you will want to obtain professional opinions from those who know your child. The first step would be to consult your pediatrician (see the section "When You Are Concerned About Your Child's Development").

In general, children's large muscle movement and gross motor skills develop faster than their fine muscle movements and finger dexterity. Receptive language (i.e., words/vocabulary children understand) is much higher than expressive language (the words they are able to speak). Thinking skills coincide with language—concrete understanding and expression develop before abstract concepts and reasoning. Children are egocentric or "me" oriented before they are able to think about others, share, and interact cooperatively.

The following lists are compiled from a variety of sources, including a number of books on early childhood development and Internet searches using the key phrase *developmental milestones*. Consider the milestones listed as rough estimates or approximations of your child's growth and development.

Developmental Milestones of 3-Year-Olds

BY THE TIME THEY HAVE THEIR FOURTH BIRTHDAY, MOST CHILDREN:

- Stand on one foot for up to five seconds
- Hop in place on one foot
- Climb upstairs and downstairs without support
- Catch a bounced ball
- Catch a ball with arms extended forward
- Throw a ball underhand
- Ride a tricycle
- Gallop
- Walk on a line

- Draw a square
- Draw a circle/face
- Draw a person with three parts
- Copy some capital letters

- Build a tower of up to nine small blocks
- Put together a simple puzzle of a few pieces
- Stack blocks or rings in order of size
- Roll balls and snakes with clay
- Button/unbutton large buttons

- Can attend to a group activity for approximately 10 to 15 minutes
- Share when asked to
- Enjoy playing tag and other active games with simple rules
- Like doing things for themselves
- Take turns with help/prompting
- Begin cooperative play
- Like to play dress-up
- Want explanations of "why" and "how"
- Recall parts of a story
- Count up to five objects
- Understand comparative concepts such as little/big and happy/sad
- Correctly name some colors

- Distinguish between fact and fantasy
- Begin to use words with abstract meaning (happy, afraid)
- Enjoy rhyming and nonsense words
- Understand prepositions like *under, over,* and *next to*
- Use *is, are,* and *am* in sentences
- Use pronouns (*me, she, he, you, I, mine*) in sentences
- Use articles (*the, a, an*) in sentences
- Speak in complete sentences, typically four to five words in length
- Understand 1,500 to 2,000 words

Developmental Milestones of 4-Year-Olds

BY THE TIME THEY HAVE THEIR FIFTH BIRTHDAY, MOST CHILDREN:

- Stand on one foot for ten seconds or longer
- Hop around on one foot
- Do somersaults
- Gallop
- Bounce and catch a ball in hands (not against the body)
- Enjoy and do well with rhythm activities/movement
- Walk backward toe-to-heel
- Walk up and down stairs with alternating feet

- Lace shoes
- Zip clothing

- Copy a cross, triangle, and other geometric patterns and shapes
- Print a few capital letters
- Print numbers and letters from a model
- Draw a person with a body (up to six recognizable parts)
- Cut on a line with scissors

- Enjoy playing in small groups
- Play games requiring taking turns and following simple rules
- Play pretend games/make believe with dolls and toys
- Understand *yesterday* and *tomorrow,* demonstrating more sophisticated time concepts and use of present, past, and future tense in speech
- Know their name in print
- Read numbers 1 through 10

- Group objects in categories
- Draw, name, and describe familiar, recognizable objects/pictures
- Tell longer stories with a simple plot
- Learn words and actions to songs that have several verses

- Play with words, such as creating rhyming words
- Speak in five- to eight-word sentences

- Understand 2,500 to 2,800 words
- Use 1,500 to 2,000 words in speech

Developmental Milestones of 5-Year-Olds

BY THE TIME THEY HAVE THEIR SIXTH BIRTHDAY, MOST CHILDREN:

- Skip on alternate feet
- Jump rope
- Skate

- Cut out simple shapes
- Color within lines
- Paste and glue

- Sort objects

- Retell a story from a picture book
- Understand how books work (e.g., words read left to right, top to bottom, words and pictures tell a story)

- Write their name
- Copy most letters
- Trace objects
- Understand the concept of opposites
- Play simple table/board games

- Have alphabet knowledge (can identify and name letters, match upper- and lower-case letters, identify corresponding sound for the letter)
- Have beginning knowledge of how print/sound code works (words are made up of individual sounds, and sounds correspond to printed letters of written word)

- Have emerging and beginning reading and writing skills
- Understand 13,000 words

The section on "What Schools Expect of Children by the End of Kindergarten" provides the specific skills and competencies that are typically expected of children in public schools by the end of kindergarten. Some of the other sections in this book discuss how young children acquire language and literacy and academic readiness and how parents can help their children acquire these skills.

Enrolling Your Child in Kindergarten or Waiting Another Year

Many parents face an agonizing and stressful choice: Is my child ready to enter kindergarten, or should we wait another year? This is a very difficult decision to make and one that takes a lot of thought and consideration. The best answer is most likely the one that you feel in your gut is right for your child. There are different cut-off dates for enrollment into kindergarten, depending on where you live. For example, in some schools the child must turn five by September 1. In other places, the cut-off date may be in October, November, or December.

You may feel your child isn't ready for the structure of a school setting or just needs more time for growth and development. Ask if the school does any readiness screening for their entering kindergarten students. You may wish to inquire about the academic, social, and behavioral expectations for the kindergarten program and ask to see the district performance standards. Different kindergarten programs will vary in their expectations. Some are academically oriented with high expectations for studentlike behavior. Other kindergartens are more developmental in focus and have different expectations and acceptable behaviors for their students. Checking into these factors may be helpful in determining if your child is ready for a successful kindergarten experience.

Many parents, especially of boys, feel their child is simply too immature developmentally (e.g., size, academic readiness, emotional development) to be entering kindergarten and embarking on their formal school career. Others are concerned that their child isn't ready because of a late birthdate, which places the child as among the youngest in the class. Many parents prefer to wait, giving their child some extra time to develop and mature, with another year of preschool experience, before enrolling in kindergarten. This is often a wise decision.

No one knows your child better than you or is in a better position to judge your child's maturity and readiness level than you are. However, gather information and check with different sources that may help you make a more informed decision. Discuss your concerns and questions with those who spend time with your child and other children. For example, talk to your child's preschool teacher and/or day-care provider. Ask your pediatrician for his or her advice.

Visit and observe your neighborhood kindergarten classrooms and any other kindergarten programs you are considering. See how the day is structured in your school's kindergarten. One factor you may wish to consider is the length of day of the program. Do you feel your child is ready and can cope with a full-day kindergarten program that most schools now have? Will your child be able to go all day without a nap? Will your child be happy or frustrated at the end of the school day?

When making the final decision, you will do best to balance what you learn (from others you speak to, your observations, and what you read) with your parental intuition and knowledge of your own child. Once you make the decision, be comfortable with the choice you made. Don't keep second-guessing yourself, which could communicate anxiety to your child. Be confident that your decision was the right one—the best decision for your child.

Additional Help Found in This Book

Parents struggling over this decision may wish to check the sections "Developmental Milestones in 3- to 5-Year-Olds," "What Are General Kindergarten Readiness Skills?" "What Schools Expect of Kindergartners by the End of the School Year," and "How to Prepare Your Child for the Social and Behavioral Expectations of School." These sections, as well as other material you read from a variety of sources, may help you reach a decision.

What Are General Kindergarten Readiness Skills?

Each child entering kindergarten is at a different developmental level than his or her peers in various skills and competencies (e.g., verbal/language, sensory-motor [gross and fine motor, auditory and visual perception], cognitive [reasoning, thinking, problem solving], social, behavioral, academic, and general maturation skills). There is a wide range of readiness skills that each youngster exhibits since each kindergartner matures developmentally at varying rates. Each has grown up with different experiences and exposures that affect the amount of background knowledge and information acquired. Some children have had nursery school/preschool and day-care experience, and others have not. Therefore, some are more familiar with working in a group, sharing, playing, and so forth than children who have not had much exposure to their peers. Those children who are most prepared for the typical expectations of kindergarten have acquired or are close to acquiring many of the following readiness skills.

Self-Care/Self-Help/Self-Awareness

- Can independently take care of bathroom/toileting needs
- Takes care of personal hygiene (e.g., washes and dries hands; blows nose)

- Can eat independently or with minimum adult assistance (e.g., help opening milk carton)
- Can dress/undress independently (or with minimal assistance needed, such as help tying a shoe)
- Finds and takes care of personal belongings
- Knows first and last names
- Knows age and birthdate
- Knows parents' and siblings' names
- Knows home telephone number

Verbal/Language

- Can express and relate ideas, thoughts, experiences, and feelings in words
- Can verbally communicate his or her personal needs
- Can understand and follow directions with two or three steps/parts
- Can listen to a story in a group setting (e.g., circle time)
- Can follow group instructions
- Can speak in short sentences
- Asks questions (why? how? where? . . .)
- Can repeat phrases or simple sentences shortly after hearing them
- Can communicate with other children
- Can engage in conversation
- Recognizes and can name many body parts
- Can describe things (e.g., what he or she is playing, doing, or looking at)
- Knows most relationship words (e.g., *above, under, next to, inside, below, around*)

- Shows interest in learning new words and in word play (joining in repetitive patterns or verse heard frequently, picking out and supplying rhyming words)

Perceptual

- Can recognize and match shapes that are the same/different
- Can recognize and match colors that are the same/different
- Can recognize and match most letters or numerals that are the same/different
- Can distinguish difference in sizes
- Can distinguish between different sounds (e.g., identifying environmental sounds, identifying which spoken words are the same or different)
- Can hear and identify sounds and words that rhyme

Motor

- Can run, climb, jump, hop, skip, and do other large muscle motor activities
- Can do activities involving eye–hand coordination (bounce a ball, catch and throw a large ball, build with blocks, string beads, manipulate smaller objects)
- Can hold and use a crayon and pencil and scissors
- Can draw a person and basic shapes (circle, square, rectangle, triangle)

Cognitive and Academic

- Has interest in stories and books
- Is beginning to understand story structure (beginning, end, main characters)

- Is beginning to understand the connection between oral language and written language (print represents words the child hears and/or says)

- Can count by rote (at least to 10—usually higher but with errors in sequence)
- Understands basic beginning number concepts (counting and one-to-one correspondence, numeral recognition)
- Can recognize simple patterns (e.g., red/blue/red/blue)
- Has some awareness of time, measurement, weather, and other general concepts

- Recites the alphabet by rote in sequence (with a few errors)
- Recognizes some alphabet letters, both capital and lower case; can name them and tell the corresponding sound

- Has interest in trying to communicate messages in writing/drawing (scribbles, draws pictures, tries copying some words or writing some random letters to communicate message or story)
- Can recognize a few words in print (including his or her name and some common words found in the environment, such as STOP)
- Is interested in and attempts to write his or her name

Social/Adaptive/Behavioral

- Can interact appropriately and function in a large group
- Can interact appropriately and function in a small group
- Comfortably interacts with children and adults

- Can work/play independently
- Can sustain attention to a task for a reasonable amount of time (approximately ten to fifteen minutes)
- Respects property of others

- Can adapt to different settings and transitions (changes in activity/routine)

- Plays cooperatively
- Participates in activities
- Shares and takes turns
- Copes with anger/frustration without excessive inappropriate behaviors, such as hitting, having tantrums, and/or running away

- Follows adult directions
- Follows rules and general routine
- Understands difference between work time and play time
- Can make simple choices (e.g., A or B)

What Schools Expect of Kindergartners by the End of the School Year

Two major emphases in education as we enter the twenty-first century are accountability *and* high standards for all. To achieve these goals, content and performance standards for every grade level, kindergarten through twelfth grade, must be established in school districts. In the recent past, expectations of students were stated in general vocabulary—for example, "Student will develop ability to . . ." or "Student will show readiness in . . . ." Expectations now are more specific and state precisely what the student will be able to *demonstrate* the ability to do. This is helpful for most teachers as it provides a clearer and more focused guide for curriculum and instruction. Another benefit of having performance standards at each grade level is consistency from school to school, classroom to classroom. For example, a student in Mrs. Smith's class in Webster Elementary School can be expected to be taught more or less the same content and skills as a student in Mr. Walker's class at another elementary school in the same school district.

Language Arts Performance Standards

The following language arts performance standards (in reading, writing, speaking, and listening) are from different school districts in the United States from East Coast to West Coast. There will be some variations in academic standards and expectations in districts across the United States. You should become aware of the standards for your child's school district, as they may differ from those listed here. However, in general, the expectations for many children *at the end of kindergarten* are that they can demonstrate the following competencies.

READING PERFORMANCE:

- Identify front cover, back cover, and title page of books.
- Hold book right side up, and turn pages in the right direction.
- Follow words from left to right and from top to bottom.
- Identify the differences between the roles of author and illustrator.

- Distinguish letters from words.
- Point out the space between words.
- Point to words with one-to-one matching—follow text as read by pointing to each word with finger.

- Identify their own name.
- Identify and name all upper-case alphabet letters.
- Identify and name all lower-case alphabet letters.
- Identify the sounds of most letters of the alphabet.
- Locate a matching word in text (find *dog*).

- Recognize words that rhyme (*fun/sun*—yes; *red/rug*—no).
- Supply a rhyming word to one heard (e.g., when hears word *map,* says *cap* or *lap).*
- Recognize words that start with same sounds (e.g., *sun/sit).*
- Recognize words that end with the same sounds (e.g., *bag/wig).*
- Identify beginning sounds in words (hears *goat,* says */g/).*
- Understand that sounds are represented by letters.
- When a single-syllable word is pronounced (e.g., *fun),* identify or segment the separate sounds by saying each sound/phoneme aloud *(f-u-n).*

- Blend sounds/phonemes that are spoken separately (e.g., *l-i-p*) to make a meaningful one-syllable word *(lip)*.
- Recognize and create rhymes.
- Respond to graphophonic cues (e.g., "Does that word look right?").
- Respond to semantic cues (e.g., "Does that make sense?").
- Respond to syntactic cues (e.g., "Does that sound right? Do we talk that way?").
- When shown letters of alphabet in isolation, give the common sound associated with most of the letters.
- When hearing a dictated sound (e.g., /b/), write the corresponding letter.
- Use knowledge of letter sounds to figure out a few simple, regularly spelled single-syllable words (e.g., *hat, pig, ran)*.
- Read with guidance and adult previewing some simple texts (beginning-level books) containing common letter/sound correspondences and familiar high-frequency words.
- Read some (approximately 25) high-frequency words that are recognized by sight (e.g., *the, you, said, he)* both in and out of context.
- Use onsets-rimes to recognize and create new words (e.g., given the word *hat* which has the onset *h* and the rime *-at,* can recognize new words *pat, rat,* and so on).
- Use pictures to make predictions about the story content.
- Use prior knowledge from own experience to talk about the text.
- Identify setting and characters.
- Retell familiar stories using beginning, middle, and end.
- Distinguish real from make-believe.
- Respond to simple questions about what is read.
- Give reactions to the book with back-up reasons.
- Make predictions based on some portions of the story.

- With books/texts they have heard read several times and are familiar with, can repeat the words with fluent intonation and appropriate pauses.
- When rereading a familiar book, monitor and self-correct when necessary (when words read don't make sense, when words don't match the picture, etc.).
- Retell story in own words or reenact in some way, getting the events in the right sequence.
- Create artwork or a written response that shows comprehension of the story that has been read.
- Listen to/read/experience works from a range of genres or categories, such as literature (stories), poetry, how-to books, and at least five different authors.

WRITING PERFORMANCE:

- Write across the page (left to right) and down the page (top to bottom).
- Write their own name.
- Write the letters of the alphabet.
- Write with pictures, letters, and "invented" (temporary or developmental) spelling.
- Represent words frequently with initial consonant sounds.

- Produce a response to literature, demonstrating understanding of literature through writing and pictures.
- Produce a narrative account (e.g., writing or dictating a language experience story). Narrative may be only a single event or several events as they move through time.
- Produce a report/informational writing (e.g., writing an "all about" book)—drawing pictures, writing/dictating information, and maintaining focus on the topic.
- Produce functional writing (e.g., label places/things in the environment, writing invitations, lists, messages, directions) with invented spelling, pictures, and so on.

- When given the materials, time, and place, write without resistance.
- Use letter approximations, letter strings, drawings, and other graphic representations to communicate meaning in writing.
- Independently create text with words that an adult can decipher.
- Reread own writing/text, matching words they have written with words they say.
- Use words in their writing that they use when talking, usually shown phonetically.
- Use words in their writing from books read to them.
- Choose words that convey their meaning.
- When reading orally, match some of the phrasing and rhythms of literary language.
- Write daily.

SPEAKING, LISTENING PERFORMANCE:

- Express ideas in complete sentences.
- Take turns respectfully when listening and speaking.
- Describe common objects and events in both general and specific language.
- Speak audibly.
- Differentiate between questions and statements.
- Follow simple two-step directions.

Mathematics Performance Standards

Standards will vary from district to district, and you should obtain a copy of your own school district's standards for the kindergarten level. Performance standards ensure that certain skills and concepts are taught. This does not mean that all children are developmentally ready to master these skills. By the end of kindergarten, students should be able to demonstrate their ability to do the following:

- Count objects up to 12.
- Count by ones up to 31.
- Count backward from 10.
- Count by twos up to 10.
- Skip-count by fives and tens to 50.

- Identify written numerals from 0 to 31.
- Select the correct numeral to indicate a quantity from 0 to 9, trace over, and write the numeral.
- Identify ordinal positions from 1st to 5th using concrete objects.
- Compare two sets of 10 or fewer concrete items and identify one as containing *more, less,* or *the same* as the other set.
- Divide a set of 2, 4, 6, 8 concrete objects into equal halves.

- Identify a penny, nickel, dime, quarter, and one-dollar bill.
- Identify the cent sign and write amounts to 9 cents using the cent sign.

- Identify one more and one less for numbers from 1 to 9.
- Add and subtract whole numbers using up to 10 concrete items.
- When prompted by a picture or situation, identify whether things would be added or subtracted.
- Identify and interpret plus and minus symbols.

- Sort objects by attribute (e.g., color, shape, size) and identify the attribute.
- Find the element of a set that does not belong and explain why it does not belong.
- Identify and describe patterns of symbols, shapes, and objects.
- Extend and create simple patterns of symbols, shapes, and objects.

- Identify the instrument used to measure length (ruler).
- Identify the instrument used to measure weight (scale).
- Identify the instruments used to measure time (clock, calendar).

- Identify the instrument used to measure temperature (thermometer).

- Make direct comparisons or use nonstandard units to measure length/height (shorter, longer, taller), weight (lighter, heavier), temperature (colder, hotter).

- Compare the volumes of two given like-shaped containers by using concrete materials (e.g., marbles, sand, water, rice).

- Tell time to the nearest hour, using analog and digital clocks, and demonstrate understanding of morning, afternoon, and night.

- Describe and tell time using calendars (e.g., days of the week, months of the year, seasons).

- Identify, describe, and draw or construct two-dimensional geometric objects (circle, triangle, square, rectangle) in the environment (e.g., clock faces, doorways).

- Notice and talk about quantities in the environment (e.g., "How many students are wearing red? brown? blue?").

- Collect information and record the results, using objects, pictures, or picture graphs.

- Identify situations in which the answers to questions such as "How many? How many more? How many all together?" can be obtained by counting, adding, or subtracting.

- Restate in their own words problems involving counting, adding, or subtracting small quantities.

- Make up problems that can be solved by counting, adding, and subtracting.

- Identify true and false statements involving the use of *either, and, or,* and *both.*

- Show understanding of the quantitative terms *all, some,* and *none.*

- Use appropriate mathematical vocabulary.

- Show ideas with a variety of concrete materials (connecting cubes, pattern blocks, buttons, beads, color tiles, etc.) and by pasting paper representations of materials.

- Explain strategies used in solving problems and share ideas orally when probed by the teacher, or when dictating to an adult for recording.
- Understand and follow oral directions for appropriate mathematics activities.

If you are concerned about your kindergartner's progress toward achieving the kindergarten grade-level standards, talk to your child's teacher. *Follow the teacher's lead and guidance* as to how you can best help and which skills to reinforce and practice at home in various ways. Do not take it upon yourself to teach your child to these standards. The standards are provided here as a general reference to increase your awareness of what teachers are teaching. Since each child develops skills at different rates, pushing your child to perform to these standards could be detrimental to a child's self-confidence and esteem.

PART 2

Creating a Learning Environment Where Children Feel Confident

This part of the book focuses on what parents can do to foster a positive, nurturing, and secure home environment for their child—one that encourages exploration and stimulates learning. Some of the best gifts we can give our children besides our unconditional love, support, and caring include our attention, our positive values and messages, the wonder and joy of stories, positive discipline and structure, and the opportunity for lots of play, fun, and interesting activities.

Every person has his or her own unique learning style differences and preferences. Young children are real hands-on learners. They are little creative beings—explorers, artists, discoverers, inventors. They thrive on exposure to music, rhythms, and movement activities. See sections *What Are Learning Styles?; Recognizing and Nurturing Your Child's Strengths and Interests; The Importance of Music, Art, and Movement/Dance Activities;* and *Developmentally Appropriate Games, Books, Songs, Manipulatives, and Other Activities/Resources* for lots of fun ideas and ways to help your child.

How children feel about themselves—their sense of competence, confidence, and self-esteem—plays a major role in every child's school success. It affects how they approach new learning, how willing they are to take risks, and how they accept inevitable mistakes from which they learn and grow. See *Building Your Child's Confidence and Self Esteem* that addresses this topic. The section on *Valuable Resources for Parents* contains a very comprehensive list of web sites that has a wealth of information and activities specific to early childhood, as well as disability and literacy organizations.

The Most Important Gifts You Can Give Your Young Child

What do children need most from us as parents? They need to feel secure and confident that we love them *unconditionally*. They need us to notice them and pay attention to them. They need us to protect them, comfort them, and provide an environment that is safe, nurturing, and conducive to learning. They need us to accept and appreciate them and sincerely believe them to be capable, competent, and good. Our children need to know that we treasure our time with them in spite of our often busy lives and numerous demands on our time. They need to be able to trust us and their other care providers. They need to know that they can count on us—that we will be there, loving, supporting, and caring for them always. The following are among the five best gifts we can give our children.

1. Your undivided attention

Young children often chatter away, talking constantly and asking questions nonstop. It isn't possible to give *all* the attention our children demand of us. Parents often feel guilty as they catch themselves pretending to listen, often responding with short answers ("uh-huh"), trying to get some peace and quiet. Even though we can't take the time to give full attention to our children as often as we would like to, it is a special gift to do so for some amount of time every day. We need to stop our other activities and try to block out distractions so we can really listen to, observe, respond to, talk with, and give our full attention to our child. Listen to what your children have to say and what they are thinking and wondering about. Observe how they play, approach new tasks, and interact with others. Respond to their questions thoughtfully, eliciting as much language and conversation as possible.

2. Play, fun, and interesting experiences

This age range from 3 to 5 years old is a time of tremendous developmental growth in your child's life. Your child is learning many new skills, vocabulary, and information about the world each day. Playing with your child—whether it is outdoor play (e.g., on playground equipment, trikes/bikes, balls, water games and activities) or indoor games (i.e., developmentally appropriate board games, building blocks and puzzles, make-believe play with puppets, dolls, action figures, stuffed animals)—is extremely valuable in many ways. Through playing together, you are providing your child the individual attention he or she thrives on. Games and activities are important learning experiences. They develop your child's gross motor skills, fine motor skills, language, cognitive/thinking/reasoning skills, and cooperative/social skills.

Children love when their parents are playful and silly and laugh with them. They learn a lot when they are involved in everyday household activities such as cooking, laundry, shopping; talking about the task at hand; and making an interactive game out of some simple and regular activities and routines. Visiting places—taking little excursions where your child is exposed to new sights, sounds, and experiences—is extremely educational and rewarding.

3. The wonder and joy of stories

Children who are read to on a regular basis become better readers, gain literacy skills more rapidly, and are more successful in school. What more precious gift is there to ourselves and our children than the intimacy and pleasure of snuggling together as we read a favorite book or share a story? The most important way to introduce your children to the world of books is through reading aloud to them every day. The act of sitting together while both you and your child are looking closely at the book, viewing the words and pictures, bringing voice to the characters and life to the words on the page, is a critically important way to instill in your child the love of reading and the motivation to become an independent reader. Stories stir the imagination, transmit important lessons and values, take us places we have never been, and let us view the world from others' viewpoints. Stories bring excitement, humor, and delight into our lives. They are comforting. They reflect that everyone has challenges to meet, and they show us repeatedly that conflicts and problems can be resolved in different ways.

When you read to your child and take the time to talk about what you read, you have the opportunity to share much more than just the story itself. By reading aloud frequently with your child, your child learns over time a lot about the difference between oral and written language and comes to understand how books work. The language of books includes vocabulary that is beyond that which your child typically uses and hears daily. This expands language development and knowledge of different concepts. Letting your child choose books to read, even when it is the same one repeatedly, gives your child a decision-making opportunity.

In addition to reading books to your child, it is another wonderful gift to tell stories to your child. Make up a story as you go along. The story line doesn't have to be sophisticated. Children love to hear stories you invent about a character and the events that happen to the character. Often they request a saga that continues with the next adventure of whichever character you created. Your child will also love to hear real stories about yourself when you were little, about Grandma, Grandpa, or other family members when they were younger.

Children are tolerant and forgiving if you aren't the most fluent reader or creative storyteller. They will listen and guide you. Just your interaction and interest, and the love you communicate through the act of sharing stories, is priceless!

4. Positive discipline and structure

Discipline is an important part of parenting. Some people think disciplining means punishing a child. But discipline actually means teaching appropriate behavior. We must be aware of our expectations for our children and never assume that they know how to behave in the ways we would like them to. Children of all ages need us to be clear on our expectations. We need to communicate them, model them, and teach them with clarity. We need to reinforce positively by recognizing and sharing our appreciation when we observe our children performing those positive/appropriate behaviors (e.g., "I noticed how you waited so patiently for your turn." "I appreciate how you didn't interrupt me when I was talking on the phone." "Thank you for helping me set the table!"). Be observant of your child's appropriate behaviors and positively reinforce those behaviors. It is also important for our children to know what is unacceptable behavior and to teach them by our firm and consistent actions that certain behaviors will not be tolerated. Providing positive discipline for our children takes a lot of work on our part. In order to be effective we must first be the loving, caring, and nurturing adults whom our children want to please.

It is important that parents' expectations of children are developmentally appropriate and reasonable. For example, children between 3 and 5 years old have a very limited ability to sit quietly. They are naturally busy and active. Most can't follow more than one or two directions at a time. Often, we need to go directly to them when we want them to listen to our direction and not call across the house, expecting them to pay attention and follow through.

An expectation such as "clean up" is meaningless unless we teach children just what "clean up" looks like. This means teaching your child that "clean up" means "toys in the toy box, books on the shelf," and so forth. First do the task together, and then observe as your child performs the task independently with your praise and encouragement.

Children thrive on structure in their lives. Predictability and routines give children security in knowing more or less what to expect. Young children often like rituals surrounding daily activities (e.g., bedtime routine, mealtime routine, getting-ready-in-the-morning routine).

5. Your positive values and the messages you give

In the formative years you teach your child consciously or unconsciously much about your values and expectations. You transmit powerful messages (intentionally or not) that affect how your child feels and thinks about self, others, and the world. As parents, we need to be aware of how we communicate to our children—our tone of voice, the words we choose, and the nonverbal (body language) we are using. Children observe us closely and learn from us how to cope with frustration; deal with anger and strong feelings; show our happiness and affection; treat others with respect; be patient, kind, honest, and cooperative. Children are astute and perceptive. They are well aware when we are insincere and don't practice what we preach.

We share positive messages and teach important prosocial behaviors and character traits by our example and by talking about situations while reading books together and guiding our children in day-to-day problem solving. Among the greatest gifts we can give our children is the message that we believe in them: noticing, recognizing, and being proud of their efforts and achievements, and encouraging them when they meet challenges. Children need to see that learning means working hard at something without fear or shame when we make mistakes.

Creating a Home Environment That Encourages Success

Above all, children need to know without a doubt that they are loved, cared for, and treasured for who they are. The home is where children need to feel the most comfortable and safe (emotionally, physically, etc.). In addition to being a place of nurturing, the home is also a place for nourishing—that is, feeding a child in every way with values, stimulation, encouragement, and opportunities to grow and develop.

Children need a certain degree of structure in their lives and in their homes. They do not do well when the environment—either home or school—is chaotic or unpredictable. Structure does not mean rigidity and strictness. Structure means letting children know their boundaries. It means simple and reasonable rules and expectations, and consistent follow-through.

In addition to simple rules, children need basic routines and schedules. There is safety and security in knowing more or less what to expect on any given evening (e.g., approximate time for dinner, bath, bedtime). In school, as well, teachers need to post a schedule (in pictures and perhaps a word or two) that shows the flow of the day. This predictability of schedule and routine gives children a sense of control in their lives. Of course, we need to be flexible, and sometimes we aren't able to follow the schedule as planned. This is fine, as children are very adaptable. It does help, however, to prepare them and let children know in advance when there will be changes in the routine.

A positive home environment allows your child the freedom to do those things that are necessary for learning and developing: playing, building, creating, exploring, inquiring, and experimenting. As adults, we may be "neatniks" who want our home to stay neat and orderly, quiet, and organized. But children are going to be noisy; they are going to make a mess. Try to be more tolerant of the disorder that comes with pulling out toys, dress-up clothes, and so on. Have a sense of humor as your child goes about the business of early childhood.

The following suggestions will help make your home a place in which your child will flourish:

• If you are able to do so, find some area in your house or basement in which your child can paint and do crafts where the mess isn't a problem for you.

• A home environment that is most conducive to a child's acquisition of social and interpersonal skills and healthy emotional development is one in which the child experiences and observes family members treating each other with respect; managing their own anger and frustrations; and being kind, cooperative, and tolerant of each other.

• A home environment that fosters literacy and a love of learning is one in which the children are surrounded by books and other print, see their parents and other family members reading for pleasure and many other purposes, associate reading and writing with comfort and joy through parents' interactions with children (e.g., sitting on a parent's lap while being read a favorite book), and so forth. Many sections in this book address ways to encourage and foster literacy in the home.

• Design and arrange your child's environment with the goals of childproofing wherever necessary (for safety and to protect valuable property), and encouraging your child's desire for independence and self-help skills. For example, put within your child's reach those things he or she needs easy access to (e.g., clothes in lower drawers, clothes hanging on lower bars in closet, plastic glasses and dishes in lower cabinet in kitchen).

• Help your child organize his or her room for ease in locating, using, and cleaning up his or her belongings. Label shelves, containers, drawers, etc., with pictures showing what belongs in or on them. Color-coding will also help your child know where to find and place belongings (e.g., the blue shelf, the red box).

• The sound of laughter, play, and music are the sounds of a home that is designed for success.

• The best home climate is one in which all family members, including your child, are able to relax, feel comfortable and at ease, and feel secure.

Building Your Child's Confidence and Self-Esteem

To be successful, children need to experience and internalize positive feelings about themselves as capable and competent learners, as being lovable and having self-worth, and as valued, respected, and cared-for individuals. These are the ingredients of a positive self-image and self-esteem.

This positive perception of self is what gives your child the confidence to take risks and try new experiences. Learning requires risk taking and not being afraid to make mistakes. A child with a positive self-image is more willing to persevere and keep trying a challenging task.

As a parent, you have the most significant influence on how your child perceives himself or herself. Children's self-esteem is in great part a reflection of how they perceive that you view them. When you show your child in your words and actions how proud you are to be his or her parent and acknowledge and praise his or her efforts, improvements, and accomplishments, you bolster your child's self-esteem.

Parents need to communicate to their children in every way that they are loved unconditionally for whom they are. Children don't need to earn the love of parents—it should be a given. Parents need to be their children's biggest cheerleaders and encouragers. Knowing Mom and Dad believe in them gives children the self-confidence to believe "I *can* do it."

It is important to enable children to do things for themselves that they are capable of, such as some simple chores or tasks that can be done independently or with minimal assistance. When we are in a hurry and are losing patience, it is much faster and easier to take over the responsibility and do the task ourselves. Avoid doing so. Allow your child the time needed to accomplish the task on his or her own. This sense of independence and accomplishment fuels your child's self-esteem.

Another key ingredient for positive self-esteem is respect. Children need to feel that they are respected, just as adults want and expect respect from children. You demonstrate respect for your son or daughter when you (a) ask your child's opinion about how he or she thinks or feels about something; (b) provide your son or daughter with choices (e.g., "Would you like to wear your green striped shirt or your blue shirt?" "Do you want a peach or a banana?"); (c) correct misbehavior with words and actions that are not demeaning, sarcastic, or critical; (d) listen to your child carefully; and (e) model respectful language and attitudes toward others.

Encourage your child to express his or her feelings. Young children often need help learning the vocabulary for labeling their feelings ("I'm angry" . . . "That makes me feel sad" . . . "I'm excited" . . . "I'm worried."). Children feel validated when you acknowledge their feelings.

Most of us feel good about ourselves when we do something nice or helpful for someone else. Instill in your child the value of being kind and supportive to others. For example, provide art supplies for your child to make a picture or get-well card for someone special who is sick, or with your child deliver blankets, clothes, or toiletries to a homeless shelter. This, too, helps build self-esteem.

The messages you communicate—your encouragement and positive expectations—are important to your child's developing self-image and self-confidence. Give your child many opportunities to experience success—goals within reach that are achievable with effort. Recognize and appreciate your child's efforts: "You really worked hard on that." "Wow, that wasn't easy." "I see what a good worker you are." Encourage your child: "I'm proud of how hard you are trying." "You can do it." "I have confidence in you." "It's tough, but you'll be able to do it soon." These are powerful words and messages, and your child should hear them often.

Be forgiving and don't overreact when your young child misbehaves, breaks or spills things, makes a mess, and so forth. Communicate that it's fine to make mistakes . . . we all do (including Mommy and Daddy). Children aren't expected to behave perfectly all of the time. Respond to and correct misbehaviors but don't make a big deal out of them. This, too, helps develop a healthy sense of self-worth. When children misbehave and you are not happy with their behavior, it does not mean that they are bad boys or girls and you don't like them. Make sure your children know this.

Protecting and Influencing Your Impressionable Young Child

Young children are very impressionable. In their innocence and naivete, they believe what they hear grownups say. They are influenced by what they see "big people" doing—especially those adults and older children with whom they live and look up to. Children will pick up and often imitate the language and behaviors of their role models. As parents, we want to surround them with as many positive role models and influences as possible. It is also our job to limit their exposure to and buffer them from models that we view as negative or harmful.

We will know what our children are doing, how they think and feel about things, and who or what they are being influenced by when we are attentive to them—observing, talking and playing with them whenever possible, monitoring and supervising, being involved and actively engaged in their activities. We need to do so, even as working parents with busy schedules. Our presence in their lives is vital. Children need to know that their parents are very interested in them.

There is much in an adult environment that is inappropriate for young, impressionable children. When we have young children, the home needs to become a child-friendly, family environment—one filled with entertainment, books, language, and activities that are geared toward the needs and interests of developing children. This means creating an atmosphere in which children are free to play, explore, make noise, and entertain themselves with developmentally appropriate toys, puzzles, blocks, balls/equipment, and so on. Preschoolers and kindergartners should be encouraged to view TV programming for early childhood audiences and listen to music in the home that includes songs that delight little children. To show our children the joy and importance of reading and writing, we need to surround them with books and provide materials to encourage them to write, draw, paint, and so forth.

Most important, children need your engagement and involvement. Play with your child. Find things to do together that are enriching and in which you will be interacting with your child. For example, go to the park together as opposed to just going to a movie. Read and tell stories to your child. Have fun. Be silly. Laugh. Slow down. Relax. Treat yourself as well as your child to special time together.

No one is more influential in the lives of children than their parents. Like it or not, what we say and how we say it makes a difference. We need to pay attention to our words. Children feel the moods and emotions of their parents. When we are having difficulty coping with problems in our own lives, we need to do our best to seek the help we need to deal with our problems. It isn't fair to take out our stress, frustration, or anger on innocent children. We need to make every effort to be positive and cheerful around our kids.

Your child's world should be a safe playground for growing and developing. As parents, we should try our best to shelter our young children from stress, anxiety, and adult problems. We need to be sensitive and gentle with their feelings and give them the gifts of childhood: innocence, wonder, excitement, and a home in which they feel secure, nurtured, protected, and loved.

One of the greatest responsibilities of parenthood is transmitting our values to our children. What children see their parents do communicates those values the most powerfully. The value of lifelong learning is transmitted best by parents and grandparents who are seen by their children as learners—seeking information and the answers to questions or problems, making the effort to learn new skills and improve in their abilities, pursuing their interests with passion, and, of course, being readers and writers.

We can't be hypocritical with children. If we tell them something is important and that we value it (e.g., reading or being respectful to others), but don't demonstrate that behavior ourselves, the message children receive is that it isn't really all that important or my parents would be doing it. Our verbal message to children is meaningless if we don't practice what we preach.

What Are Learning Styles?

How do children learn that it is all right to be different—to learn, think, and approach problems in different ways? How do they come to accept others and recognize that we all have strengths in some areas, weaknesses in others? Children learn that we all have our differences—which are to be respected and appreciated—by what they hear and observe from us, parents and teachers. They learn by our example and what we communicate to them, beginning in the early childhood years and throughout their childhood and adolescence. This may be one of the most important lessons we ever teach our children if we hope they will grow up to be adults with tolerance and empathy for others, individuals capable of developing positive relationships in their lives and working successfully in a global society. Among the many differences we all have, part of what makes each of us unique is our own learning style.

Teachers trying to reach and teach to the learning needs of all the students in the classroom incorporate learning style theory and awareness into instruction. Basically, learning styles refer to the fact that we all learn in different ways. There isn't one approach that is going to work with everyone. Each of us takes in and processes information through different modalities or sensory channels: auditory—by hearing it; visual—by seeing it; tactile-kinesthetic—by touching, moving, doing it. Many of us are stronger and learn better through one modality over another, and we tend to have preferences in our learning styles.

If your child is a keen listener, remembers things well that he or she hears, has strong interest and talent in verbal games, and does very well with rhyming and blending activities and word games, your child may be a strong auditory learner. If your child is very observant and seems to learn best when watching, remembers very well when seeing pictures, and tunes in to visual details, he or she may be a strong visual learner.

People who are strong tactile-kinesthetic learners learn by doing, touching, and moving. They are hands-on learners who need to be involved physically with projects and activities. Of course, preschoolers and kindergartners are all developmentally hands-on active learners. As children mature and get older, many remain predominantly tactile-kinesthetic learners; others show learning preferences that are auditory or visual; others have a fairly balanced and even modality preference.

In the absence of physical disabilities or a sensory impairment (e.g., deafness, blindness), we all are able to learn through multi-modalities (auditory, visual, tactile-kinesthetic modes). Teachers recognize that to be most effective, it is best to instruct using a multisensory approach, which means that children should be given input when learning that involves hearing, seeing, and being actively involved, with the opportunity to touch and move. Also, children need to be able to demonstrate what they know through a variety of learning styles (e.g., through song, dance, writing, speaking, constructing, role playing, and reenacting).

It is helpful for parents, as well as teachers, to be aware that children's learning styles may be different from their own. Just as each child has a different temperament and personality, each child's approach to learning will also differ. It is important that we nurture the development of all the modalities and help our children feel comfortable learning new things in a variety of ways.

Learning styles involve other factors, such as how we are affected by sound (e.g., some of us like and do our work well with music in the background, others do not); where we work best (e.g., some of us need to work at a table/desk, others are more productive and comfortable working on the floor or other area). This is something to keep in mind as your child gets older. Generally, at a young age your child will spend a lot of play and work time on the floor. Developmentally, staying seated very long or sitting at a desk or table isn't what young children do. However, it is recommended to have a child-sized table or desk and chair in the house where your child's feet should touch the floor when seated. Your child should use this desk or table when trying to write properly.

Recognizing and Nurturing Your Child's Strengths and Interests

One of the joys of parenthood is observing the exuberance of our child's play, the thrill of a new discovery, the look of pride on our child's face when mastering a new skill. Life is full of wonder and excitement when we live with a young child! As our children play and participate in different activities, their interests and competencies develop. It is fun as a parent to discover our child's interests and talents. Of course, children move from one interest and fascination to another. By listening and talking to your child, observing his or her play, and watching what holds your child's attention the longest, you should recognize his or her interests and aptitudes. It is important to nurture and cultivate those budding interests and any strengths/talents your child exhibits.

We help our children develop by providing a variety of experiences. Those experiences related to something the child is interested in are very motivating and reinforcing. For example, if your child is interested in airplanes, it is a thrill to go to or near an airport and watch the planes take off and land. If your child is interested in tigers or bears, an outing to the zoo together is a valuable experience.

The following activities will help you learn about and develop your child's strengths and interests:

- Play ball with your child. Of course, when old enough to play team sports, your child will most likely be very excited to join a T-ball or soccer team.

- Teach your child how to swim. This is a very important skill for safety as well as sport and fun. Try to do this as early as you can.

- Encourage your child to build collections or at least most of them. Help find containers and books for your child's collected rocks, shells, leaves, cards, and so forth.

- Foster your child's imagination and interest in make-believe/creative play by providing the materials—for example, unused cartons for making forts, etc.; old clothes, scarves, shoes for dress-up; empty food boxes/containers and kitchen utensils to play shopping, restaurant, cooking.

- Keep a scrapbook of your child as he or she grows through the preschool and kindergarten years. You will find the pictures that you take of your child engaged in his or her favorite activities, with the crafts he or she makes, and during the grand performances (music and dance) in your living room for friends and family to be priceless treasures in a few years.

- Provide your child with music—children's songs and simple toy instruments. Play a variety of music in your home.

- If your child is interested in dance, encourage this interest through exposure to different dance forms (e.g., ballet, tap, jazz) and consider a dance class at some point.

- Have available in your home the supplies/materials/equipment needed for an activity. For example, your little artist will need crayons, paper, paints, easel, etc. Your builder needs blocks of different types and sizes. Your paleontologist needs shovels for digging and lots of dinosaur books.

Most important, show interest in what your child expresses interest in. Reinforce those interests by talking about them, reading about them, and providing your support and encouragement. Your young child has many years ahead to explore his or her interests and develop new strengths and talents. It is best not to push young children into too many activities and lessons/classes. Your child is perfectly happy and content playing at home and in the neighborhood, and is learning through playing.

The Importance of Music, Art, and Movement/ Dance Activities

Three- to five-year-olds are exuberant little learners, as they make new discoveries and acquire new skills and competencies every day. As discussed in the section "What Are Learning Styles?" children learn best when they experience through *all* their senses—hearing, seeing, touching, feeling, moving, smelling.

Sadly, there tends to be much less emphasis and opportunity for the creative and performing arts in education as children move up in the grades. When there are budget cuts in school districts, art, music, and drama are always the first areas cut from the school program or course offerings. This is unfortunate because much is to be gained by providing musical and artistic experiences throughout a child's educational journey.

Fortunately, preschool and kindergarten curriculum is heavily embedded with music, art, and movement (e.g., marching, dancing, acting things out). These are very critical components of an effective preschool and kindergarten program.

Music

Children learn much by hearing music of different kinds. They learn to discriminate between different sounds, pitches, and rhythms. They learn to identify rhymes, which are so common in the lyrics of songs.

Rhyming is critical to the development of phonemic and phonological awareness. Children learn rhythm, which is important in skills such as counting, patterning, and many gross motor activities.

Music speaks to our emotions. It can positively affect our mood. Music can be uplifting and make us feel good. It can also be calming, soothing, and comforting. It can energize us or relax us. The opportunity to hear and play different instruments builds good auditory discrimination and listening skills. It is also a strong motivator and means of self-expression.

Art

Art—in the form of drawing, painting, and crafts—fosters growth in many developmental skills. Many fine motor skills are involved in art activities, such as squeezing glue, using a finger to paste, holding a scissors to cut, and holding and controlling pens, crayons, paint brushes. Children learn many basic concepts through art such as color, design, patterning, size/shape, directionality, and borders and boundaries. Numerous visual-perceptual skills are developed through arts and crafts—discriminating and attending to the likenesses and differences in shapes, size, color, position in space.

Movement/Dance

Dancing and marching help children develop in many ways. They improve a child's sense of rhythm and beat. They are fun and social experiences. They build math concepts (e.g., counting with one-to-one correspondence of the movement matched simultaneously to the count, patterns such as step-step-kick, step-step-kick). They develop a child's coordination, motor control, and balance. They develop laterality—the awareness within the body of the difference between right and left. These activities also develop a child's spatial perception and directionality, which are necessary in reading and writing (e.g., recognizing and producing letters that look similar but are rotated in space, such as *b/d/p/q; m/n;* reading and writing with left-to-right progression).

Creative movement activities (e.g., waddle like a duck, gallop like a horse, slither like a snake, hop like a frog, crawl like a baby) help children develop in many ways. Besides motor skills, these activities increase children's vocabulary, develop thinking and association skills, and expose children to the language of similes and metaphors (descriptive language they hear in books and poems and will begin to incorporate in their own writing).

Being able to control, imitate/copy, and remember a sequence of large motor movements, such as follow the teacher's lead in some simple dance steps or movements, is very important. It is prerequisite to being able to control, copy, and remember a sequence of smaller motor movements necessary for writing letters, words, and numbers.

One of the best ways we can help our children be successful in school and life is to provide them with an outlet for their energy (positive and negative), for their creativity, and for their feelings. Nothing does that better than music, art, dance, and sports of various kinds. These are necessities in life and essential for one's well-being. They nourish the heart and soul. They are therapeutic. They are positive and healthy outlets for letting off steam, stress, or anxiety; channeling energy; and expressing the gamut of emotions.

It is a gift to provide your child from a young age with exposure to the various art forms. Through these experiences many children will develop their strengths and interests, which are critical to a happy life. (See the section "Recognizing and Nurturing Your Child's Strengths and Interests.") As parents, it is our role to introduce our children to the many possibilities that exist but to allow our children the freedom to pursue and explore to their hearts' content.

Developmentally Appropriate Games, Books, Songs, Manipulatives, and Other Activities/Resources

Preacademic Skill Development

Alphabet Bingo (ages 4+) by Trend

Alphabet Match Me Game (ages 3–6) by Trend

ABC Match Ups Puzzle Set by Lakeshore

Alphabet Adventure (ages 3+) by Lakeshore

Colors and Shapes Bingo (ages 3+) by Trend

Colors and Shapes Match Me Game (ages 3+) by Trend

Numbers 0–10 Match Me Game by Trend

Number Match Ups Puzzle Set by Lakeshore

Make-a-Pattern Puzzle Set by Lakeshore

Puzzle Set—Simple Sequence (ages 3+) by Lakeshore

Make-a-Word Picture Puzzles (ages 3+) by Lakeshore

Sound It Out Picture Puzzles by Lakeshore

Memory Match—Word Opposites by Frank Schaffer

Basic Skills Puzzles—Opposites by Didax Educational Resources

Basic Skills Puzzles—Sound Alike by Didax Educational Resources

Judy Clock (age 4+) by Judy/Instructo

Sesame Street ABC Desk by Fisher Price

Hug and Learn Little Leap (ages 2–5) by Leap Frog

Phonics Desk Learning Systems (ages 3–8) by Leap Frog

Fun & Learn Phonics Bus (ages 18 months–4 years) by Leap
Frog

Sesame Street Games—Big, Small, Short, Tall (ages 3+) by
Fisher Price

Green Eggs & Ham (ages 4+) by University Games

The Cat in the Hat Game (ages 4+) by University Games

Manipulatives for Fine Motor, Perceptual Development, Creativity, and Eye-Hand Coordination

Fabulous Fiddlestix—rod and connector toy set (ages 3+) by
Toys-N-Things

Wedgits—3D blocks by RC Products (1998 Toy of the Year,
Parenting magazine)

Gears! Gears! Gears! Building Set by Learning Resources

Legos by Lego Company

Lincoln Logs by K'Nex

Wood Number Blocks by Tootsie Toy

Foam Building Blocks by Grand Toy

Jumbo Plastic Lacing Beads (ages 3+) by Ideal

Jumbo Plastic Nuts & Bolts by Ideal

Lace a Person (ages 5–9) by Lauri

Lace a Pet by Lauri

Other lacing activities (Swamp Creatures, Crawling Critters,
Lace a Saurus) by Lauri

Lace, Trace 'n Play Animal Friends (ages 3–6) by Trend

Lace, Trace 'n Play Transportation by Trend

Lace, Trace 'n Play Seasonal Shapes by Trend

Busy Bugs Lacing Shapes Cards (ages 3+) by Ideal

Jigsaw puzzles of various kinds (e.g., floor puzzles, jumbo puzzles—wooden, crepe rubber, and other materials)

Magna Doodle (ages 3+) by Fisher Price

Etch-a-Sketch (ages 4+) by Ohio Art

Lite Brite (ages 4+) by Hasbro

Favorite Games

Scrabble Junior (ages 5+) by Milton Bradley

Ants in the Pants (ages 3–6) by Milton Bradley

Cootie (ages 3–6) by Milton Bradley

Don't Spill the Beans (ages 3–6) by Milton Bradley

The I-Spy Game (ages 4+) by Living & Learning

Boggle Junior (ages 3–6) by Parker Brothers

Candyland (ages 3–6) by Milton Bradley

Chutes and Ladders (ages 3–6) by Milton Bradley

Hi Ho Cherry-O (ages 3–6) by Milton Bradley

Monopoly Junior (ages 5–8) by Parker Brothers

Yahtzee Junior (ages 4–6) by Milton Bradley

Popomatic Trouble (ages 5+) by Milton Bradley

Perfection (ages 5+) by Milton Bradley

Memory Game (ages 3–6) by Milton Bradley

Mr. Potato Head Says (ages 3+) by Hasbro

Hungry, Hungry Hippos (ages 3+) by Milton Bradley

Card Games: Old Maid, Go Fish

Favorite Nursery Rhymes, Action Songs, and Fingerplays

Georgie Porgie

Humpty Dumpty

Twinkle, Twinkle, Little Star

Baa Baa Black Sheep

Old King Cole

Mary Had a Little Lamb

Little Boy Blue

Hey Diddle Diddle

Ring Around the Rosies

Pat-a-Cake

This Little Piggy

Jack and Jill

Hickory Dickory Dock

Old MacDonald

Little Miss Muffet

Three Blind Mice

Little Bo Peep

Oh Where, Oh Where Has My Little Dog Gone?

One, Two, Buckle My Shoe

Wheels on the Bus

Five Little Monkeys

We're Going on a Bear Hunt

Hokey Pokey

If You're Happy and You Know It

Itsy Bitsy Spider (or Eency Weency Spider)

This Old Man

There Was an Old Lady

Good Morning to You

The Old Gray Mare

Hush Little Baby

Are You Sleeping?

Polly Wolly Doodle

A Tisket, a Tasket

Rain Rain Go Away

Animal Fair

Yankee Doodle

The Ants Go Marching

Teddy Bear, Teddy Bear

Educational Software Companies

Didax Educational Resources

Edmark (**www.edmark.com**)

The Learning Company (**www.learningco.com**)

Great Wave Software

Broderbund Software, Inc. (**www.broder.com**)

Lego Media International (**www.legomedia.com**)

Disney Interactive (**www.disneyinteractive.com**)

School Zone Interactive

Creative Wonders

Knowledge Adventure

Hasbro Interactive

Favorite Rhyming Books

Cat in the Hat by Dr. Seuss, New York: Random House, 1957

Hop on Pop by Dr. Seuss, New York: Random House, 1963

Green Eggs and Ham by Dr. Seuss, New York: Random House, 1960

One Fish, Two Fish, Red Fish, Blue Fish by Dr. Seuss, New York: Random House, 1960

Polar Bear, Polar Bear, What Do You Hear? by Bill Martin, Jr. & Eric Carle, New York: Henry Holt & Co., 1991

Chicka Chicka Boom Boom by Bill Martin, Jr. & John Archambault, New York: Simon & Schuster for Young Readers, 1989

Brown Bear, Brown Bear, What Do You See? by Bill Martin, Jr. & Eric Carle, New York: Holt, Rinehart & Winston, 1989

Is Your Mama a Llama? by D. Guarino, New York: Scholastic, 1989

Other Books

FOLK TALES—*Goldilocks and the Three Bears, The Three Billy Goats Gruff, The Three Little Pigs, The Little Red Hen, Little Red Riding Hood*

CONCEPT BOOKS—alphabet, colors, counting, farm animals, jungle animals, weather, seasons. Examples include:

Color

Color, Color, Color, Color by Ruth Heller, New York: Putnam & Grosset, 1995

The Mixed-Up Chameleon by Eric Carle, New York: HarperCollins, 1991

Of Colors and Things by Tana Hoban, New York: Greenwillow, 1989

Counting

Ten, Nine, Eight by Molly Bang, New York: Mulberry, 1983

Waving: A Counting Book by Peter Sis, New York: Greenwillow, 1988

One Gorilla: A Counting Book by Atsuko Morozumi, Farrar, Straus & Giroux, 1990

Ten Black Dots by Donald Crews, New York: Greenwillow, 1986

Fish Eyes by Lois Ehlert, San Diego: Harcourt Brace Jovanovich, 1990

Alphabet

Gathering the Sun, An Alphabet in Spanish and English by Alma Flox Ada, et al., New York: Lothrop, Lee & Shepard, 1997

An Animated Alphabet by M. Angel, New York: David R. Godine, 1996

The Cowboy ABC by Chris Demerest, New York: DK Publishing, 1997

Eating the Alphabet by Lois Ehlert, New York: Harcourt Brace, 1989

The Amazing I Spy ABC by Ken Laidlaw, New York: Dial Books, 1991

V Is for Vanishing, An Alphabet of Endangered Animals by Patricia Mullins, New York: HarperCollins, 1993

K Is for Kiss Good Night: A Bedtime Alphabet by J. Sardegna, New York: Picture Yearling, 1996

Children's Magazines

Ladybug
The Cricket Magazine Group
www.ladybugmag.com
P.O. Box 7436
Red Oak, IA 51591–2436

Sesame Street
www.ctw.org/sesame
Children's Television Workshop
One Lincoln Plaza
New York, NY 10023

Your Big Back Yard
www.nwf.org/ybby
National Wildlife Federation
8925 Leesburg Pike
Vienna, VA 22184

Other Favorite Toys

- Young children love musical toys such as drums, xylophones, bells, keyboards, and so forth. They also love any dress-up clothes, playsets, and props that encourage imaginary play.
- Children also love ride-on vehicles of all kinds (e.g., tricycles, fire engines), balls of different sizes, and other toys/equipment that involve active play and enhance the development of coordination and gross motor skills.

Recommended for Parents

Hey! Listen to This—Stories to Read Aloud edited by Jim Trelease, New York: Penguin Books, 1992

American Library Association Best of the Best for Children edited by Denise Perry Donavin, New York: Random House, 1992

The New York Times Parent's Guide to the Best Books for Children by Eden Ross Lipson, New York: Times Books–Random House, 1991

Words, Words, Words—A Reference Book for Beginning Writers with Rhyming Dictionary by Babs Bell Hajdusiewicz, Glenview, IL: A Good Year Book, 1997

Finger Rhymes by Marc Brown, New York: Dutton, 1980

The Raffi Singable Songbook by Raffi, New York: Crown, 1987

Read-Aloud Rhymes for the Very Young by Jack Prelutsky, New York: Knopf, 1986

Tomie dePaola's Mother Goose by Tomie dePaola, New York: Putnam, 1985

American Folk Songs for Children by Ruth Crawford Seeger, Tucson, AZ: Zephyr, 1970

The Random House Book of Mother Goose edited by Arnold Lobel, New York: Random House, 1986

The Random House Book of Poetry for Children edited by Jack Prelutsky, New York: Random House, 1983

Best Web Sites for Kids 2000 by Jessica Shroeter, New York: Teacher Created Materials, Inc., 2000

The Internet Kids & Family Yellow Pages by Jean Armour Polly, Berkeley, CA: Osborne/McGraw-Hill, 2000

Ask in libraries and bookstores for favorite and recommended titles of books (particularly the Caldecott Medal and Newbery Medal winners) in the categories of wordless books, picture books, and story books. See the section "Valuable Resources for Parents," which lists numerous web sites that will help children to learn and grow.

Valuable Resources
for Parents

The following organizations, associations, and centers provide a tremendous amount of information on a wide range of topics important to parents. Many are government-sponsored web sites whose purpose is to provide the latest, up-to-date information and support to the public. Take the time to browse the web sites. Look for the links to parent information and resources, early childhood pages, and so forth. You will find a goldmine of valuable information for helping your child succeed in school and answers to just about any possible parenting question. This section also includes an extensive resource section addressing various disabilities—with information, guidance, and supports to parents of children with special needs.

Literacy

Association for Library Service to Children
www.ala.org/alsc
50 East Huron Street
Chicago, IL 60611
800-545-2433 ext. 2163

American Library Association
www.ala.org/parents/index.html
50 East Huron Street
Chicago, IL 60611
800-545-2433

Center for the Improvement of Early Reading Achievement
www.ciera.org
University of Michigan School of Education
610 E. University Ave., Rm. 1600 SEB
Ann Arbor, MI 48109-1259
734-647-6940

Children's Book Council
www.cbcbooks.org
12 W. 37th Street, 2nd Floor
New York, NY 10018
212-966-1990
800-999-2160 (Order Dept.)

Committee on the Prevention of Reading Difficulties
   in Young Children
National Research Council, HA 178
2101 Constitution Avenue NW
Washington, DC 20418
202-334-3462

ERIC (Educational Resources Information Center) is a national information system designed to provide users with access to an extensive body of education-related literature. It is supported by the U.S. Department of Education, the Office of Educational Research and Improvement, and the National Library of Education.

ERIC Clearinghouse on Reading, English, and Communication
www.indiana.edu/~eric_rec
Indiana University
Smith Research Center, Suite 150
Bloomington, IN 47408-2698
800-759-4723

ERIC Clearinghouse on Elementary
    and Early Childhood Education
ericeece.org
University of Illinois Children's Research Center
51 Gerty Drive
Champaign, IL 61820-7469
800-583-4135

Internet Public Library Youth Division
www.ipl.org/youth
4172 Shapiro Undergraduate Division
University of Michigan
Ann Arbor, MI 48109-1185
(Go to Fun Stuff for Pre-Schoolers)

International Reading Association
www.reading.org
800 Barbsdale Road
P.O. Box 8139
Newark, DE 19714
302-731-1600
800-336-READ

National Association for the Education
    of Young Children
www.naeyc.org
1509 16th Street NW
Washington, DC 20036
800-424-2460

National Head Start Association
www.nhsa.org
1651 Prince Street
Alexandria, VA 22314
703-739-0875

National Institute on Early Childhood Development
    and Education
www.ed.gov/offices/OERI/ECI

National Parent Information Network
npin.org
Larry Yates
Columbia University Teachers College
525 W. 120th Street
New York, NY 10027
800-601-4868

U.S. Department of Education
READ*WRITE*NOW Activities for Reading and Writing Fun
www.ed.gov/inits/americareads
800-USA-LEARN

U.S. Department of Education Publications
www.ed.gov/pubs/parents.html
U.S. Department of Education
400 Maryland Avenue SW
Washington, DC 20202
800-USA-LEARN

Headsprout Reading
www.headsprout.com

An early literacy program designed for teaching children (4–6 years old) letter/sounds, systematic phonics, and other beginning reading skills through interactive games and cartoon episodes via Internet access at home.

Web Sites for Children and Families

ABC's of Parenting
www.abcparenting.com

Disney's Family.com
www.family.com

Early Childhood Educators' and Family Web Corner
users.sgi.net/~cokids

The Family Education Network
www.familyeducation.com

50+ Great Sites for Kids & Parents
www.ala.org/parentspage/greatsites/50.html

Hall of Early Childhood Education
www.tenet.edu/academia/earlychild.html

KidsConnect
www.ala.org/ICONN/kidsconn.html

Kids Online
www.kidsonline.org

Kids Online: Protecting Your Children in Cyperspace
www.protectkids.com

Little Explorers
www.EnchantedLearning.com/Dictionary.html
206-232-4880

Netparents
www.netparents.org

Parent-Child Home Program
www.parent-child.org

Parent's Picks Web Sites
www.parentsoup.com/onlineguide/parentspicks/web.html

Parent Soup
www.parentsoup.com

PBS home-schooling page
www.wsbe.org/Education/Pointers/homesch.html

Mr. Rogers' Neighborhood PBS Online
www.pbs.org/rogers/

Safekids.com
www.safekids.com

Sesame Workshop
www.sesamestreet.org/

SmartParent.com
www.smartparent.com

Top 10 Internet Sites for Families
www.ala.org/ICONN/topten.html

Resources on Disabilities and Special Needs

AskERIC (Educational Resources Information Center)—a free question answering service provided by ERIC. Submit any questions about education, parenting, and child development for an e-mail response within two working days: **askeric@askeric.org**.

Asthma and Allergy Foundation of America
800-727-8462

Autism-PDD Resources Network
www.autism-pdd.net

Autism Society of America
www.autism-society.org
7910 Woodmont Ave., Suite 650
Bethesda, MD 20814-3015
800-328-8476

Children and Adults with Attention Deficit Disorder (C.H.A.D.D.)
www.chadd.org
8181 Professional Plaza, Suite 201
Landover, MD 20785
800-233-4050

Council for Exceptional Children
www.cec.sped.org
1920 Association Drive
Reston, VA 22091-1589
800-232-7323

ERIC Clearinghouse on Disabilities and Gifted Education
1920 Association Drive
Reston, VA 22091
800-328-0272

The International Dyslexia Association
(formerly The Orton Dyslexia Society)
www.interdys.org
Chester Building, Suite 382
8600 LaSalle Road
Baltimore, MD 21204

LD OnLine: An Interactive Guide to Learning
    Disabilities for Parents, Teachers, and Children
www.ldonline.org.

Learning Disabilities Association
www.ldanatl.org
4156 Library Road
Pittsburgh, PA 15234
412-341-1515

National Alliance for the Mentally Ill
www.nami.org
200 North Glebe Road, Suite 1015
Arlington, VA 22203–3754
800-950-6264

National Information Center for Children
    and Youth with Disabilities
www.nichcy.org
P.O. Box 1492
Washington, DC 20013
800-695-0285

National Information Center on Deafness
www.gallaudet.edu/~nicd
Gallaudet University
800 Florida Avenue NE
Washington, DC 20002-3695
202-651-5052

*National Institute of Child Care
  and Human Development*
U.S. Department of Health and Human Services
31 Center Drive
Building 31, Room 2A32
Bethesda, MD 20892-2425

*The National Library Service
  for the Blind and Physically Handicapped*
Library of Congress
Washington, DC 20542

*Office of Special Education
  and Rehabilitative Services*
U.S. Department of Education
Washington, DC 20202

Parents Helping Parents
www.php.com

Recordings for the Blind and Dyslexic
www.rfbd.org
20 Roszel Road
Princeton, NJ 08540

*Schwab Foundation for Learning
(formerly Parents' Educational Resource Center)*
www.schwablearning.org
1650 South Amphlett Blvd., Suite 300
San Mateo, CA 94402
800-230-0988

Tourette Syndrome Association, Inc.
tsa.mgh.harvard.edul
4240 Bell Blvd.
Bayside, NY 11361
800-237-0717

Miscellaneous

The American Academy of Pediatrics
www.aap.org
601 Thirteenth Street NW
Suite 400 North
Washington, DC 20005
800-336-5475

American School Directory
www.asd.com
P.O. Box 20002
Murfreesboro, TN 37129-0071

National Parent Teacher Association (PTA)
www.pta.org
330 N. Wabash Avenue, Suite 2100
Chicago, IL 60611
312-670-6782
800-307-4PTA (4782)

Partnership for Family Involvement in Education
pfie.ed.gov
U.S. Department of Education
400 Maryland Avenue SW
Washington, DC 20202-8173

National Child Care Information Center
www.nccic.org
243 Church Street, NW, 2nd Floor
Vienna, VA 22180
800-616-2242

National Institute of Child Health and Child Development
www.nichd.nih.gov
Bldg. 31, Room 2A32, MSC2425
31 Center Drive
Bethesda, MD 20892-2425
800-370-2943

PART 3

Advice on Social, Behavioral, and Discipline Issues

One of the most important responsibilities we have as parents is to teach our children how to behave appropriately, get along with others, and be responsible. Discipline means teaching, and we do this through our clear expectations, effective communication, guidance, enforcement of limits, and follow through. Structure and boundaries give children a sense of security and safety. These sections address how to parent using effective positive discipline—strategies that are proactive rather than reactive, encourage cooperation, and are known to have long-lasting results. Moreover, they foster a positive, loving, and respectful relationship between you and your child.

Most early childhood teachers will tell you that appropriate social and behavioral skills (e.g., listening, following directions, sharing, taking turns, being able to display self-control) are more important for school success than academic competence. As your child's first and primary teacher, you can do a lot to help your son or daughter develop these critical skills. Strategies and suggestions will be provided in the sections *Communicating So Your Child Will Listen Better and Pay Attention, How to Prepare Your Child for the Social and Behavioral Expectations of School, Effective Behavioral Strategies and Positive Discipline Practices,* and *Developing Your Child's Problem-Solving Skills and Ability to Get Along with Others.*

It is best to be able to prevent behavioral problems whenever possible. Many can be avoided by using our awareness of our child's needs and tolerance levels (e.g., physical, emotional), planning ahead and preparing, and setting up an environment that is supportive of our child's needs. The section *Preventing Behavioral Problems at Home and Other Places* addresses this topic.

Some children are more behaviorally challenged than others. They may be highly active, far more so than most children of their age. They may have an extremely low tolerance for certain environments (e.g., crowded and noisy places like department stores and malls). They may be excessively demanding. They may not listen or comply with adult directives or requests. Some children have neurobiological reasons for their more extreme and challenging behaviors (e.g., those who may have ADHD—attention deficit hyperactivity disorder). Other children are also challenging in their behaviors simply because of their individual personalities and temperaments. See the section *Tips for Parenting Challenging Children* for suggestions and strategies on this topic.

Communicating So Your Child Will Listen Better and Pay Attention

No one enjoys being interrupted when absorbed in an activity of choice. It is especially hard for a young child to stop playing in order to do something he or she may not wish to do (e.g, "Come to the table" or "Put your toys away"). Often it is difficult to get your child to listen when you speak and do what you ask. The following tips and strategies will help your child listen and pay attention:

• Get your child's attention directly before giving directions. This means face-to-face and direct eye contact. Don't expect your child to pay attention when you give directions from across the house.

• You may need to walk over and touch your child gently to get his or her attention and eye contact before giving a direction.

• If your child is very focused on a TV show, you may need to turn off the TV before trying to give your child an instruction or direction.

• Keep directions clear, brief, and to the point. Adults tend to talk too much when giving directions to children. State what you want your child to do with as few words as possible ("Please, put your shoes on now.")

- Once you have your child's attention and state your direction, stop talking. Again, adults have the tendency to keep on talking and not allow the child a chance to comply.

- Give your directions whenever possible by saying what you want your child to do, not what you don't want your child to do. It is better to say, "Sit on the couch" rather than "Don't jump on the couch" and "We walk in the house" rather than "Don't run in the house."

- Another strategy is to give a direction and have your child repeat or rephrase what he or she is supposed to do. This checks your child's understanding of the direction. Then wait and watch to see that your child starts to do what you ask.

- Give directions that are statements, not questions. Say, "Lights off in ten minutes." Don't say, "Are you ready to turn off the lights?"

- Young children can't remember more than two or three things at a time. Many children can only follow a one-step direction. So break down directions into small steps of what you want your child to do.

- Make routines and schedules visual for your child. A helpful technique is to draw pictures or cut pictures out and mount them on a chart that will be posted in a visible and convenient place for your child to see and reach. The picture chart shows the sequence of the morning routine/activities or evening routine/activities. For example, the top section of the chart can show a picture of clothing to indicate getting dressed. The second section may have a picture of a cereal bowl or various breakfast foods to show eating breakfast. The third section can show a picture of a hairbrush and toothbrush to indicate grooming. As your child completes each task, he or she moves a clothespin down the chart to attach next to the corresponding picture.

- Give frequent praise and positive feedback when your child follows directions and/or is making a good attempt to do so. Thank your child for being cooperative.

- Young children respond well to making a game out of any chore or task you want them to do. For example, set challenges: "Let's see if we can put the blocks back in the basket by the time we count to ten (or by the time this song ends)."

If we want children to develop good listening skills, we need to practice and model what it looks like and sounds like to be a good listener. Being able to listen to the teacher, classmates, and others is a critical part of school learning and a fundamental readiness skill. You can model good listening behaviors for your child by doing the following:

- Be patient when your child struggles to express himself or herself. Give your child the chance to put his or her thoughts into words. Try not to finish children's sentences for them in an attempt to speed them along in what they have to say.

- Good listening means showing interest by making and maintaining eye contact, responding to what someone is saying, and being an "active listener." For example, you can ask questions for more information, paraphrase what the speaker said, or make comments related to what the speaker said.

How to Prepare Your Child for the Social and Behavioral Expectations of School

Most kindergarten teachers will say that it isn't as important how far a child can count, or how many alphabet letters a child may know (and other academic readiness skills) upon entering school compared with the child's social and emotional readiness. One of the many advantages for children who have had preschool experience is their exposure to the social and behavioral expectations of kindergarten and future grades. This includes the ability to do the following:

- Show interest in and interact appropriately with other children
- Interact and communicate with different adults
- Share with others

- Follow simple directions
- Comply with adult requests/directives
- Wait and take turns

- Function appropriately and cooperatively in a large group
- Function appropriately and cooperatively in a small group
- Be able to work and function independently for a reasonable amount of time
- Handle transitions and changes in routine
- Follow rules

- Get along with others
- Show a reasonable degree of self-control and self-management (e.g., of anger)
- Show willingness to participate and try new things

- Say "please," "thank you," "excuse me"
- Listen to others politely
- Respond to others and to verbal questions
- Express self and needs verbally
- Engage in conversation

- Independently handle personal care needs (e.g., toileting, feeding, dressing)
- Attend to task for short amount of time
- Finish a short task

- Handle property of self and others appropriately
- Show willingness to help others and accept help/assistance
- Understand nonverbal cues (e.g., shaking head "no," quiet down signal of finger to lips)
- Show concern and empathy for feelings of others
- Behave nonaggressively with others (e.g., hands and feet to self)
- Understand and adapt behavior to the environment (know difference between acceptable volume for the classroom, "inside voice" and "outdoor voice")
- Play in friendly manner with other children

Once children are in day-care, preschool, and kindergarten environments, the demands and expectations are quite different from those of being at home. Your child is now one of a group and must learn to cooperate and behave in ways that are socially acceptable and appropriate. To promote social and emotional readiness, invite other children over to your home to play. Give your child opportunities to engage and interact with other small groups of children in a variety of different activities. Play games with your child in which he or she needs to share and take turns. This is a perfect time for you to model how to play fair, how to be a good sport when losing, and so forth.

Some children have physiological factors that underly their weakness with many social and behavioral skills (e.g., those with ADHD, a neurobiological disorder making their ability to control or inhibit their impulses and regulate their activity level much more difficult). Some children have personalities and temperaments that are challenging. Some youngsters are immature or lacking in social or behavioral skills because they haven't been provided enough modeling and teaching of these skills. For others, the behavioral and social expectations of a school setting are completely foreign to them and differ greatly from the expectations in their home and in other environments in which they have grown.

It helps to prepare your child for the positive social and behavioral expectations of school and life by exposing your child to a number of social situations, observing his or her behavior closely, and modeling and guiding your child in positive, prosocial skills. Take the time to teach appropriate behaviors and ways to be a friend, be a listener, be a helper, and so forth. This is a very important role of parenting and one that makes a tremendous difference in the life of your child. Those children who are socially competent and mature in their behavior (e.g., better self-control) are generally happier and more successful in and out of school than those who are not.

Effective Behavioral Strategies and Positive Discipline Practices

An important part of parenthood is disciplining our children and teaching them appropriate behaviors. Discipline is not the same as punishment, even though sometimes as parents we do need to punish (or give negative consequences to) our children for their unacceptable behaviors. What discipline means is *teaching* children what is acceptable and unacceptable behavior—teaching them the behaviors we want them to display through the use of positive and negative consequences. Throughout childhood, adolescence, and adulthood, those who have the best chances for success in school, in the workplace, and in life have developed the self-discipline to work hard, persevere, exhibit self-control, and seek their goals. They have learned how to adapt to and function in different environments and behave in ways that are socially acceptable in those environments.

Parents need to start at the earliest ages in helping children learn these important skills. There are different modes of discipline that parents utilize, many of which we have acquired from our own parents' discipline techniques. The following are principles of effective positive discipline—strategies and understandings that are known to have the best long-lasting results and foster a positive, loving, and respectful relationship between you and your child.

SETTING THE FOUNDATION

• Establish a few specific, important rules or expectations that are clearly understood by all members of the household. These are usually related to aggressive and disrespectful behavior.

• Set limits and boundaries. Your child needs to know what is unacceptable and that you mean business and will enforce those limits consistently.

• Provide structure, routine, and predictability in the home. Children do not function well in a chaotic environment. Knowing that there is a general routine and flow to their life, as well as clear limits, provides the sense of security, safety, and peace of mind children need to be healthy and happy.

POSITIVE REINFORCERS

• Pay attention to your child when he or she is behaving in appropriate ways. A key behavioral principle and one we generally ignore or forget is that behavior that is reinforced (attended to in some way, either positively or negatively) is the behavior that will be repeated. This is probably the most powerful and important thing we can do and something that most adults—parents and teachers—unfortunately neglect to do. The tendency of adults is to notice and interact or respond in some way to children when they are misbehaving because that's what gets our attention. Children may be engaged in positive, desirable behavior (e.g., playing cooperatively and sharing with siblings) for a long period of time. We don't tune into this positive behavior. We don't say anything to them or notice them during this time. As soon as there is a problem such as arguing, or one starts crying or hits the other, we notice and begin interacting by scolding or removing them from the situation.

• Positively and immediately reinforce your child when you see him or her engaged in desirable behavior. Positive reinforcement means doing something or providing something that your child likes (e.g., praise, smiles, hugs, a treat, a privilege or special activity, stickers toward earning something). Positive reinforcements encourage the behavior and increase the likelihood that it will be repeated. Use the smallest reinforcer necessary. In most cases, attention and positive reinforcement through smiles, hugs and kisses, specific praise, compliments, and acknowledgment will be enough. For example, "You cleaned that up by yourself—great job!" "I noticed how you two are sharing and taking turns. I'm so proud of you!" "Cameron, I appreciate how you didn't interrupt when I was talking to Mrs. Smith. You showed good manners."

• Children love and respond to material or tangible treats (e.g., small toys, snacks, trinkets, books, puzzles). Fun activities and special attention are also powerful reinforcers (e.g., a piggyback ride, high five, playing a game together, an outing such as to the beach/park/restaurant/ice cream shop). Inviting a friend over or spending time with a special person like Aunt Nancy and other privileges (e.g., staying up a few minutes later than normal bedtime, selecting a meal for lunch) are also great motivators.

• At times, especially in elementary school, you may wish to use a token economy system. This involves giving a token of some kind like stickers or smiley faces when a child earns it for a particular behavior. These tokens are accumulated and "cashed in" or redeemed for another reinforcer that is very motivating to the child. If your child makes a huge fuss every night when it is time to take a bath or shower, you may wish to try making a very simple chart such as a piece of construction paper cut out in the shape of a bunny with three or four half-dollar-sized circles drawn on it. Tell your child that every time he or she takes a bath without a fuss, he or she will get to put a sticker inside a circle on the bunny chart. When the chart has all of the circles filled with stickers, your child earns a special treat. Together you agree on what that will be (e.g., "Daddy will take you for a bike ride").

• When your child is in school and is having behavioral problems, it is often helpful to work out a system between the home and school for positive reinforcement. For example, if your child has been hitting other children, he or she can go home at the end of the day with a card that has a big smiley face or sticker on it and the words "I didn't hit. I kept my hands to myself." Parents would supply the positive reinforcer for "no hitting" or "kept hands to myself" days.

CONSEQUENCES FOR NEGATIVE BEHAVIORS

- Negative consequences (or punishments) also work in changing behavior. Children must know that rules/limits will be enforced, and that if they choose not to follow the rules, there will be consequences. Punishments should be used, however, much less frequently than positive consequences in our parenting. There are different kinds of negative consequences that you may use. One kind is a verbal reprimand. For example, "Shoes off the couch." "Stop teasing your sister." "No grabbing, ask politely." Another negative consequence can be a loss of a privilege, such as not getting to watch a desired television program or losing the privilege of temporarily playing with a favorite toy.

- When verbally correcting a misbehavior, it should be done without yelling, screaming, hostility, or too many words. Use a tone of voice that is calm, businesslike, and nonemotional. It is important to separate the behavior that you are unhappy with from the child. Be careful not to say things that state or imply that your child is a bad person. Keep in mind that with all children, especially very young ones, lecturing or talking too much is not effective.

- "Do overs" or "Try it agains" are another form of correcting inappropriate behavior. It basically involves requiring the child to redo the inappropriate behavior the correct or appropriate way. It gives the child another chance to make a better choice. For example, if your child asks for something rudely, say, "Try that again by asking me politely." If your child slams doors shut, and has been asked before not to do so, say, "That's not how we close doors. Do it again, please."

- In most cases it is not wise to ignore misbehavior. The behaviors that do respond well to ignoring are attention-getting behaviors like whining. Pay absolutely no attention to the child when engaged in this behavior. When the misbehavior (whining) stops, pay positive attention to the child at that time.

- Timeout is a negative consequence. This is when you isolate the child for a brief amount of time. It is generally recommended that when using a timeout, the amount of time is one minute for every year of age. So, 3-year-olds should have timeout no more than three minutes, 4-year-olds no more than four minutes, 5-year-olds no more than five minutes, and so forth. For timeouts pick a location that is boring for your child, safe, but away from other people and activity. When the child is sent to timeout, the child remains in that location without interaction for a short, designated amount of time. When the time period passes, and if the child is calm and cooperative, he or she reenters the regular setting without any additional scolding. It is often recommended to set a timer. When the timer rings, timeout is over if the child is behaving appropriately. If the child is not yet under control, let the child simply know that the timer rang but timeout isn't over until he or she is ready to cooperate.

ADDITIONAL ADVICE

- When asking your child to do something, state the request or directive as a "do" rather than a "don't" when possible. For example: "Walk in the house, please" rather than "Don't run in the house." "Michael, clean up your blocks now, please" rather than "Don't leave your blocks on the floor."

- Children do best if they have some control and choices— even very young children. Give them limited choices. For children of this age group, let your child select between two choices you can live with (A or B). For example, "Would you like to wear the teddy bear pajamas or your fire engine ones?" "You can wipe that up with a paper towel or a sponge. Which one? You choose."

To be effective in disciplining children, we must be adults whom the child trusts, respects, and has a positive relationship with.

Examine yourself and consider the disciplinary practices you most often use. If you find that many of your interactions with your preschooler/kindergartner involve giving your attention when the child is misbehaving, if you are scolding or punishing more than praising and rewarding, now is the time to develop other more positive parenting strategies.

There are a number of excellent books and other resources on behavioral strategies and management techniques. The following are some recommended resources:

Cline, Foster, and Jim Fay. *Parenting With Love and Logic.* Colorado Springs, CO: Pinon Press, 1990.

Faber, Adele, and Elaine Mazlish. *How to Talk So Kids Will Listen and Listen So Kids Will Talk.* New York: Avon Books, 1980 (updated printing 1999).

Garber, Stephen W., Marianne Daniels Garber, and Robyn Freedman Spizman. *Good Behavior.* New York: St. Martin's Paperbacks, 1987.

MacKenzie, Robert J. *Setting Limits.* Rocklin, CA: Prima Publishing, 1998.

Nelson, Jane, Lynn Lott, and Stephen Glenn. *Positive Discipline A–Z: 1001 Solutions to Everyday Parenting Problems.* Rocklin, CA: Prima Publishing, 1999.

Phelan, Thomas W. *1–2–3 Magic: Effective Discipline for Children 2–12.* Glen Ellyn, IL: Child Management, Inc., 1995.

Developing Your Child's Problem-Solving Skills and Ability to Get Along with Others

As discussed in the section "How to Prepare Your Child for the Social and Behavioral Expectations of School," getting along with others, expressing feelings, and coping with the frustrations and challenges of life in behaviorally appropriate ways are very important skills. Parents are their children's first and primary teachers, and are responsible for teaching these skills from the early childhood years.

You can help your child develop the social skills necessary for getting along with others by providing the opportunity to practice such skills. If there are other young children in the neighborhood, allow your child the chance to play with them. It is often best to encourage play with one other child at a time, rather than a group, until your child can handle larger group play. Observe (from a distance) how your child interacts with other children. Is he or she bossy or cooperative? Is he or she too physical and aggressive? Does your child share with others appropriately? Can your child take turns and accept (without crying or having tantrums) if he or she loses when playing a game? Does your child know how to enter into play with other children—asking if he or she can join (e.g., "Can I play with you?")? Does your child speak to others with friendly words and tone of voice or could his or her words and behavior be interpreted as mean and unfriendly?

All of these social behaviors can and should be taught through modeling, talking about them, intervening and practicing correctly, and praising frequently when you observe your child exhibiting the positive behaviors you want. For example, "I noticed how nicely you shared your toys with Michael. That's being a good friend." "You waited for your turn so patiently—just like a big kid!"

When possible, take your child and a friend someplace they can play and have fun together while being physically active, preferably outdoors to a park or playground. Provide some fun, supervised activity your child and a friend can do together for an indoor activity (e.g., a craft project, decorating cookies). If your son or daughter tends to have difficulty getting along with other children, keep the play periods short. If playing at a friend's house, anticipate that your child is likely to overextend his or her welcome if playing for more than a limited amount of time. Avoid doing so by picking your child up after a certain time has elapsed and by calling the supervising parent to see "how things are going," especially for first play dates.

Children learn from us what to do when things don't go the way we wish. We model to our kids all the time how to handle frustration, anger, and other feelings. When we rant and rave and behave like a child having tantrums, that's what our children learn. We need to show them that there are other ways to solve our problems and cope with negative feelings.

It helps if we don't come unglued at every little thing. We all have bad days. We all make mistakes. We all break things. It is expected that our children will. It is best if we don't overreact, punish every little thing, and view our children's misbehaviors or mess-ups as big deals all the time. They need to know that if something goes wrong, we still love them no matter what; they need to learn that most problems can be corrected.

Children need to learn ways to solve problems and try to fix things in appropriate ways. Help them to use words that describe their feelings. For example, "That bothers me," "I don't like that," "I feel angry." Guide your child to use language for problem solving by asking leading questions (e.g., "What should you say to Lisa if that bothers you?"). The more children can view their role models using language and thinking skills effectively to solve problems, the better. It helps if they can observe older siblings and parents in control of their emotions and using problem-solving language and strategies (for example, hearing parents ask older brothers and sisters who are being disciplined questions such as "What would have been a better choice? What are you going to do differently next time?"). Most children between the ages of 3 and 5 aren't mature enough in their reasoning skills or language to problem solve to this extent, but it is good to start early in modeling and teaching these skills.

Preventing Behavioral Problems at Home and Other Places

As discussed in a previous section, "Effective Behavioral Strategies and Positive Discipline Practices," there are certain general guidelines that foster positive behavior and discipline. These include establishing and providing the necessary structure—simple rules and expectations; setting and enforcing clear, consistent limits; responding to misbehaviors with predictability, not randomly; and trying to keep calm and in control of your emotions when responding to inappropriate behaviors. Most important, you must focus most of your attention on your child's positive behaviors rather than his or her negative behaviors. Notice your child engaged in desirable behavior and provide immediate positive feedback. Do this as frequently as possible rather than waiting until misbehaviors occur and then attending to your child with negative, corrective feedback and punishment.

It is best to prevent behavioral problems whenever possible by being proactive as parents—using our awareness of our child's needs and tolerance levels, planning ahead and preparing, and setting up an environment that is supportive. It is best to set up routines and adhere to them as closely as possible. For example, you have morning routines (getting ready for school), mealtime routines (setting the table), and bedtime routines (reading a story before sleep). Changes in routines are often stress-provoking for children. At those times, it is very common for children to have difficulty maintaining appropriate behavior. Prepare your child ahead of time for changes like redecorating or remodeling your home, a change in parent work schedules, visitors or house guests, and, of course, new babies. Talk about changes and avoid surprises.

Following are strategies to consider for preventing or reducing the occurrence and/or frequency of behavioral problems in the home and other settings.

How to Maintain Good Behavior at Home

• Organize and arrange the home environment in a way that optimizes your child's chances for success and avoid failure. Remove objects you don't want your child to play with or touch. In other words, "child proof" your home.

• Purchase toys, books, games, and other play and/or learning materials that are age-appropriate for your child and not too frustrating. For example, you would not give a tool set meant for an 8-year-old to a young child who has not developed the fine motor skills and necessary hand-eye coordination to hold and use a tool like a screwdriver.

• Avoid competitive activities or prepare for games and activities that involve competition. Walk your child through the strategies of what to do if he or she loses a game. Reinforce good sportsmanship by telling and showing your child that you can't always win when playing games. When playing games, praise and reward behavior that requires your child to display self-control.

• Give your child responsibilities or simple tasks or chores to do that he or she is able to handle. Don't overdo responsibilities for your young child. When given a task or chore, make sure it is something that the child can complete in a very short amount of time. Do it together a number of times until your child is easily able to do that task or chore independently, and then be sure to pay attention and praise your child each time for a job well done.

• Be aware of siblings who are teasing and provoking one another. Intervene since young children lack the skills to handle such situations on their own. After a cooling off period, discuss what the rules are about teasing and/or aggressive behavior.

• Provide physical outlets for your child where he or she is able to release energy and participate in physical activities such as running, jumping, and climbing. These activities allow for a great deal of movement and are essential for young, growing children. See the section "The Importance of Music, Art, and Movement/Dance Activities."

How to Maintain Good Behavior Outside of the Home

• When taking your child out of the home, give him or her time to get ready and talk about what to expect. Give advance notice. Realize that any change of routine can be unnerving and stressful for children. Provide the preparation and avoid catching them off guard.

• Don't take your young child to places that you know will be too stimulating or make it difficult to manage and supervise your child's behavior. These situations can tax a child's self-control and attention span, especially when he or she is tired and needs a nap.

• Teach, model, and practice appropriate manners and behaviors you want your child to display outside the home. Before going to public places like a store, doctor's office, restaurant, or another person's home, talk to your child about the behaviors you expect from him or her. State the rules simply. Review them and have your child repeat them back to you.

• Be prepared with a "bag of tricks." Don't leave home without a variety of toys, books, audiotapes, and other items that can occupy your child and keep him or her entertained. Keep the bag of tricks fresh—change them periodically to maintain novelty and interest.

- Monitor your child's behavior. Supervise your child in other people's homes and public places. Remove your child from a situation when he or she is behaving inappropriately or showing signs of losing control.

- Give your child feedback when you are with him or her outside the home. For example, "I'm proud of how you are behaving. It looks like you'll earn the *(name reward)* that we talked about."

- Avoid taking your child to places that are geared for adult audiences or participation, where one is expected to sit and remain quiet for any length of time.

Rewards and Consequences

- Plan ahead which behaviors you will work toward increasing and how you will reward or positively reinforce those behaviors. Avoid discipline that is reactive. Plan with your partner/spouse on how to deal with certain challenging behaviors. When they occur, calmly use the strategy that you agreed upon. Don't react or respond out of anger, as we tend to, and then do or say things that we often regret later.

- Establish rewards(s) that your child will be able to receive if he or she behaves appropriately and follows the rule(s).

- Let your child know the consequences if he or she behaves inappropriately. Follow through and mean what you say.

- Talk to your child about the natural consequences of inappropriate behavior. For example, friends won't want to play with him or her and parents won't invite your child to their house.

- Avoid shopping with young children without building in the opportunity for them to earn a small treat for good behavior. It is advised not to overdo this strategy since your child might learn to expect a reward each time you shop and/or each time he or she displays good behavior.

Other Tips and Strategies

• Redirect your child's attention to something else if you observe him or her beginning to show increased negative behavior. For example, you can say "Oh, look at the bird on the tree over there" or "Jenny, let's find a book to read together." Distracting your child from the situation, changing his or her location (e.g., going outside or to another room), and redirecting him or her to an interesting task is very helpful in preventing your child from losing control and needing to be disciplined for negative behavior.

• Find baby sitters you can trust and use them. There are times when both parents and their children need time for themselves. Parents need time together to rejuvenate their relationships; children need time with other caregivers to prepare them for their independence.

• Be observant. Anticipate potential problems, stressors, and frustrating expectations at home or in other settings. Avoid or circumvent them.

• Avoid fatigue, your child's and your own. When we are tired, we have less patience and tolerance, and may say or do things that we'll regret later on.

• Maintain flexibility and a sense of humor. These can get you through some tough situations.

Tips for Parenting Challenging Children

Some children are much more behaviorally challenging than others. They may be far more active than most children. They may have an extremely low tolerance for certain environments (e.g., department stores, places with crowds or a lot of noise). They may be excessively demanding. They may not listen or comply with adult directives or requests. Parents are exhausted and weary from having to supervise their child every moment. Some children have neurobiological reasons for their more extreme and challenging behaviors (e.g., those who may have ADHD). Unfortunately, people often assume that the parents of such children aren't doing their job of parenting. Observers often assume that the child is out of control because of permissive parenting and no discipline.

Parents of children with ADHD or some other neurobiological disorders will generally have a lot of difficulty managing their child's behaviors in spite of their best efforts. Their children are far more challenging to parent than others. Often the parenting and disciplining techniques that are effective for most children don't work well with theirs.

Some children are challenging in their behaviors simply because of their individual personalities and temperaments. Parents who have more than one child know well how different each of them is in temperament. Some children are almost always smiling, cheerful, and good natured. They can occupy themselves calmly. Other children are bossy and demanding and much more difficult. They tend to have temper tantrums, cry a lot, and so forth.

Other sections of this book provide a number of strategies for helping your child develop positive prosocial behaviors. Read "How to Prepare Your Child for the Social and Behavioral Expectations of School," "Developing Your Child's Problem-Solving Skills and Ability to Get Along with Others," "Effective Behavioral Strategies and Positive Discipline Practices," and "Preventing Behavioral Problems at Home and Other Places." In addition, the following strategies are helpful:

• If your child exhibits challenging behaviors, start early in learning how to become an expert on positive behavioral strategies. Read as much as you can. There are excellent books, tapes, and other resources at the public library that can give professional advice on how to handle specific situations (e.g., your child's name calling, aggression, tantrums, noncompliance, or refusal to comply with your requests).

• When you have a challenging child, it is important that both parents work together as a team. You must carry out agreed-upon strategies for a variety of challenging behaviors. Consistency in how behaviors are dealt with is critical.

• A difficult or challenging child is often the source of marital problems and strife in the home. Parents should not blame each other but should seek professional help and be supportive of each other. This helps everyone in the home feel more positive toward each other and cope with the stress.

• If positive strategies are not working well, be sure to seek professional assistance and consultation to determine if your child has any physical and/or physiological reason for the behaviors. Talk honestly with your pediatrician. Other childhood specialists who would be appropriate to see include child psychologists or child psychiatrists and pediatric neurologists.

• Talk to professionals at your child's school, such as your child's teacher, the school nurse, the school psychologist, the school counselor, and the principal. Of course, if you are concerned about other problems your child exhibits besides behavior (e.g., immature language development, lack of readiness skills, weakness in motor and other physical skills), be sure to consult with school personnel. There are a number of specialists within the public school setting who could be of help—such as the speech/language specialist, the resource or special education teacher, the physical education and adaptive physical education teacher—in advising you and perhaps in providing service to your child.

ADDITIONAL HELP THIS BOOK OFFERS

If you suspect your child has a disability of some kind (which could be underlying the difficult behaviors), share those concerns with the school or school district. Children with disabilities are entitled to a full range of various supports and services. See the sections in "Part 6—What to Do if You Suspect Your Child Has a Developmental Delay or Disability" for further help.

PART 4

Everything a Parent Needs to Know on How Children Learn to Read

This part of the book provides you with the most current information about how young children learn to read, and what can be done to prevent reading difficulties. You can help set your child on the path of reading success with this knowledge. See the sections *Language and Literacy: The Building Blocks of School Success; What Is Phonemic and Phonological Awareness?; What to Expect in the Emergent and Beginning Levels of Reading Development; What Good Readers Do: Positive Reading Behaviors;* and *What Research Says About Preventing Reading Difficulties.*

You will find that this part of the book is packed with fun, interactive strategies and activities that will help your child develop important foundational skills for becoming a reader. See the sections *Playing with Sounds and Language; Helping Your Child Learn the Alphabet; Getting Them Off to a Good Start: Strategies for Developing Emergent and Beginning Reading Skills;* and others.

By providing your child with many of the same strategies that his or her preschool and kindergarten teacher will be using in class, you can reinforce what your child learns at school. See the sections *The Importance of Read-Alouds and Shared Reading: Strategies for Reading* to and with *Your Child; Building Vocabulary and Comprehension Skills; How to Ask Questions That Guide Your Child in Developing Good Reading Habits and Thinking Skills;* and *Beginning Phonics, Word Recognition, and Word Study Skills.*

Language and Literacy: The Building Blocks of School Success

Children have an amazing capacity for learning complex things such as language. We take it for granted that our children will acquire language and the ability to communicate. We typically don't think about having to teach our children language, as we know from experience and observation that children seem to learn this critically important skill naturally. Language is the foundation of most everything we do and learn. It is highly functional, enabling us to communicate with those around us, get meaning from our world, and express our deepest thoughts and feelings. The need to make meaning, communicate, and interact effectively with others is probably the strongest of intrinsic human motivations. There are different aspects or domains of language: oral language (speaking and listening), and the literacy domains of reading and writing. There is also nonverbal language—expressing and getting meaning through using and reading gestures/body language and signing.

According to researchers in language acquisition (Krashen & Terrell, 1983), we all acquire language, whether it is the primary language we learn as infants and young children or a second foreign language that is learned later in life, by progressing through a series of predictable stages. These stages of language proficiency include the preproduction, early production, speech emergence, intermediate fluency, and advanced fluency stages.

In general, during infancy we hear, listen, and internalize language but aren't yet producing speech. In the early years we start trying to communicate through simple speech, trying to make ourselves understood and responding with one or two words. As speech begins to emerge, we start to speak in phrases and short sentences, making many grammatical errors as we experiment with language. We soon progress into the fluency stages as our command of language develops rapidly. Without consciously being aware of it, we are now speaking in complete, flowing sentences, with correct grammar and a vast vocabulary.

It is amazing to observe your child's language development. Although the progression to language proficiency is natural, it happens at different rates for each child. Language is so important for school success that we need to do whatever we can to nurture and help our child in language development. The section titled "Playing with Sounds and Language" provides fun activities and ways you can help your child in language development. The following are the most important things you can do to facilitate language growth and development:

• Talk a lot to and with your child. Engage in conversation with your child during everyday activities (on a walk, while driving somewhere, during meals, while bathing, during play, while doing chores).

• Be a good language model.

• Ask your child questions.

• Pay attention and respond to your child when he or she is talking to you.

• Expand on the language your child is using. For example, if your son or daughter points and says, "juice," build on that by asking, "Do you want Mommy to give you more juice?" If your child says, "I losted two tooths," respond with correct grammar: "You lost two teeth? Wow! Smile and let me see."

• Read aloud every day, pointing to illustrations in the book, modeling fluency and expression when reading the words, and pausing to ask a question from time to time related to the story. ("I wonder what's going to happen next. What do you think the bear will do?")

• Point out unfamiliar objects in your child's environment and name them.

• Describe and have your child describe objects he or she sees.

• Expose your child to lots of rhyming (songs, poems, nursery rhymes, books with rhyming patterns such as the Dr. Seuss books).

• Play word games that call attention to different sounds.

• Encourage talk and play with dolls, puppets, action figures, stuffed toys.

• Encourage taking turns listening and talking.

• Play games that help focus on listening to and identifying sounds in the environment. For example, "Guess what sound this is . . ." (make a tape recording of sounds such as a horn honking, a car passing by, a siren of an ambulance or fire engine, the kettle whistling, a bird chirping, the water running, a computer booting up).

• Take your child to story time when it is offered at your local library or book stores.

• Sign up to receive information from your local children's book stores regarding special activities that promote literacy experiences (e.g., puppet shows, story hour). Children's books stores also are among the best sources of information regarding books your child will love.

Preschool and kindergarten children are at the stage of emerging literacy when they learn the connection between spoken language and written language and come to understand how words they hear and say can be recorded by written marks (letters) that are combined into groups (words) on a page. They learn that the vocabulary and language of books and stories is somewhat different from our everyday language (e.g., "once upon a time," "in a faraway land," "a brave young lad"), and they become familiar with written language. By the many experiences we give them during these developmental years, they learn how books work—how to hold a book properly, turn the pages at the right time, point to words initially while saying them. They pick up on the directionality of words going left to right and from the top to the bottom of the page. They learn how the reader's eyes (and initially finger or pointer) sweep from the end of the line when reading back to the beginning of the next line of print. They begin to understand that the words on the page have meaning and that what readers do is read for meaning. Well before children are able to read any words on a page independently, you will observe them "reading" books by going through the motions they observe readers doing. They will pick up a picture book and pretend to read. This is important developmentally in literacy acquisition.

Writing is also a developmental process that children go through. By observing parents and other writing models in their lives, they learn that we communicate in an important way through putting our words and ideas on paper. Very young children imitate our writing behaviors. If we supply the materials (i.e., paper and crayons), we will see children "writing" messages and stories. We are familiar with the scratches very young children make on a page, along with their drawings. As they learn how to form a few letters, children will write some random letters on the page. Then as they learn some letter/sound correspondence, they will string letters together to try and form words. There is a complex progression of skill development in writing involving perceptual skills, fine motor skills, letter-and-sound recognition and identification skills, and language and thinking skills.

Note: Krashen, S., and T. Terrell. *The Natural Approach.* Hayward, CA: The Alemany Press, 1983.

What Is Phonemic and Phonological Awareness?

To read and write, we have to understand that the letters of the alphabet are symbols representing sounds of speech. Phonological awareness is the understanding that speech is composed of parts, and the smallest part is the phoneme. To read or write, a child must learn that spoken words are made up of a sequence of sounds or phonemes. This isn't an easy or automatic concept for children. It means hearing a spoken word (e.g., *hat*) and being aware that it is actually made up of three separate sounds: /h/ /a/ /t/. It is the understanding that the beginning sound of *hat* is /h/ and the ending sound is /t/. It would also involve hearing the /at/ sound within the word, and recognizing other words that end with the /at/ sound that rhyme (e.g., *sat, fat, bat)*.

Within the past few years it has been found through the results of very important research that phonological awareness is absolutely critical to learning how to read. It is now known that children who have reading difficulties in first grade and higher have often never acquired the necessary auditory skills of phonological awareness needed in order to decode or read print. Phonemic and phonological awareness are actually prerequisite skills to reading.

In the preschool years children are developing their awareness of sounds in the words they hear *(phonemic awareness)* through the language activities they are exposed to that focus on sounds (e.g., rhymes, poems, songs, nursery rhymes, listening for words that start with the same sound). Once children are able to grasp the understanding and recognition of individual sounds in words, and are able to manipulate (or play around with) those sounds, they have acquired a very critical skill for becoming a reader and writer.

There has been a tremendous amount of research over the past few decades to determine how children learn to read and what can be done to prevent reading difficulties. (See the section "What Research Says About Preventing Reading Difficulties" for more information about this topic and the significance of phonological and phonemic awareness in reading development.) Fairly recently, the findings from this large body of research has become available and is being used by educators to improve reading instruction in classrooms throughout the nation. The following are some of the findings from this important research:

• Reading development requires the acquisition of phonemic awareness and other phonological processing skills.

• There is a strong association between a child's ability to read and the ability to *segment* words into sounds (phonemes) and to *blend* sounds (phonemes) into words. Segmenting words into sounds or phonemes is the ability to stretch out a word and say it slowly (e.g., saying the word *lip* slowly—*lllliiip* and recognizing that there are three distinct sounds in the word). Blending phonemes or sounds into words is the ability to identify a word when hearing the sounds of the word stretched out in sequence. For example, if you were to say to a child, *fffffuuuuunnnnn,* he or she would be able to recognize the whole word and say *fun.*

• Beginning readers need phonemic awareness in order to be able to apply phonetic strategies (phonics) for sounding out printed words. This makes sense, because you need sound awareness of speech first, before you can decode a printed word through its letter/sounds. To read, a child needs to recognize and identify the sounds within the printed word. The reader needs to start with the first sound(s) at the beginning of the word, and blend together (left-to-right) each of the following sounds matching the letter/sound combinations of the word.

• With direct, explicit instruction children can learn phonemic awareness and develop these phonological skills crucial to reading and writing.

This is valuable information for parents to be aware of. Be sure that your preschool and kindergarten programs provide many activities that promote and target the development of phonological/phonemic awareness. There are a lot of games, activities, and strategies to use at home that will help. Some are listed in the next section, "Playing with Sounds and Language." Also, see the activities under *auditory processing skills* in the section "Children with Learning Disabilities, ADHD, and Other Disabilities, Disorders, and Special Needs."

If you have concerns that your child has immaturities or delays in phonological awareness, consult with your child's preschool or kindergarten teacher, or with a speech/language specialist. Children can be screened in mid to late kindergarten to determine if there is a weakness in this area. If so, intervention in the form of one-on-one or small group instruction should be provided to help your child acquire these skills.

Some recommended software and computer programs for building these skills include:

Earobics (888-328-8199) **www.cogcon.com**

Daisey's Quest and Daisey's Castle (Great Wave Software) (800) 423-1144 **www.greatwave.com**

Headsprout Reading **www.headsprout.com**

Playing with Sounds and Language

The following activities are fun and beneficial in helping your child develop listening skills, letter/sound awareness, vocabulary, and other important language skills:

- Sing songs, calling attention to the rhyming verse and any silly word play in the songs.

- Read/share poems and nursery rhymes.

- Do finger play activities together (e.g., Eency Weency Spider).

- Read books together that have rhyming verse, repetitive patterns, and play with words (e.g., Dr. Seuss).

- Play games like "Simon Says" that specifically involve giving directions that involve prepositions and language that describe where. For example, "Simon says: Put the pillow *behind* the chair. Simon says: Walk *around* the table two times." *Note:* Use words such as *on top of, inside, under/underneath, next to/beside, above/over, behind/in back of,* and so forth.

- Play games requiring looking for and naming objects that are categorized by a certain characteristic or attribute. For example, "Let's take turns naming things that are round or shaped like a circle . . . things that are green . . . things made of wood . . . ."

• Play games such as, "I'm thinking of something you would find in a park . . . I'm thinking of something you find in a super-market . . ." For early childhood, you give the clues so the child can guess. For example: "I'm thinking of a fruit. It is yellow and you can peel it" and "I'm thinking of something you find in the kitchen. It is big and shaped like a rectangle. It is something that keeps things cold . . ." and so forth until the child guesses. *Note:* This is a wonderful game for all ages. With older children, play it in the form of twenty questions, in which the players have up to twenty opportunities to guess what the person is thinking of (by narrowing it down through well-thought-out questions). The one who is being questioned can only answer with yes or no responses. Examples of questioning: "Is it something you can eat?" (no) "Is it something made of metal?" (yes) "Is it something you can hold in your hands?" (no) "Is it something that has wheels?" (yes) The correct guess is *shopping cart.*

• Look through picture books, magazines, or any print visual media so that your child can name objects and discuss the picture or illustration with you.

• When reading with your child a familiar story (one that he or she knows pretty much by heart), pause and let your child supply words to finish some of the sentences—particularly those that complete a rhyme.

• Use any experience (baking cookies, going on a walk, excursions and everyday activities such as going together to the grocery store, bank, doctor's office) as an opportunity to talk about what happens in that environment. Use language and vocabulary words related to that place or activity.

• Expose your child to a variety of music and opportunities to hear different musical instruments.

• Dance and move to different rhythms and beats.

• Make up silly rhymes or verses to songs.

• Play numerous rhyming games and activities in which your child has to identify the words that rhyme, match pictures of objects that rhyme, tell you another word that rhymes with a word you supply, and so forth.

- Read books and play games with alliteration (using the same beginning sound in sentences or verse). For example, "Silly Sammy Seal somersaults on the sand." The repetition of the /s/ sound is an alliteration, as is the familiar "Peter Piper picked a pack of pickled peppers."

- Play games with targeted sounds: "D is for /d/—*dog.* D is for /d/—*dinosaur.* D is for /d/—*dollar.*"

- Hunt for pictures or objects beginning with a target sound. For example, make a game out of finding things that start with /b/. Together find and identify things in the environment, such as *bed, book, basket, bread,* and so forth.

- Play games such as "Say my secret word fast: /p/, /i/, /g/." Your child, after repeated practice, will eventually blend those isolated sounds/phonemes and say *pig.*

- Play games such as "I'm going on a trip, and in my suitcase I'm packing ___." Take turns naming items that begin with a certain sound. This will be silly and it is not a memory activity. *Note:* Older children can play this game by recalling and repeating the previous items in the sequence and adding a new one at the end. But young children just play to think of a word beginning with a sound. For example, "I'm packing a . . . toothbrush, television, tomato, tent, turkey . . ."

- Play games that focus your child's attention on discriminating and identifying sounds within the environment. For example, sit by an open window and both of you close your eyes. Have your child identify the sounds he or she hears (e.g., car driving by, children laughing, birds chirping, leaves rustling, car alarm going off, engine starting, lawn mower running, phone ringing).

- Have your child clap to every word he or she hears in a sentence. For example, model how to and have your child clap with you as you say one-syllable words in simple sentences. For example, "I love you" (three claps), "Joan has a new doll" (five claps). As your child progresses, add some two-syllable words to your sentences. For example, "Billy sells cars" (three claps).

• Clap to syllables in a word or name. For example, *Hannah-Han•nah* (two claps), *Amanda-A•man•da* (three claps), *Joseph-Jo•seph* (two claps). *Variation:* Say, "I'm thinking of somebody in our family whose name has three claps in it."

• Take a picture of a common object (e.g., toy monkey) and cut it into the same number of parts as there are syllables in the word (e.g., *mon•key* has two syllables, so cut the picture of the monkey into halves). As you say the word slowly, accentuating the two syllables *(mon . . . key)* have your child move the first piece of the monkey picture (head and top of body) as you say *mon,* and then the second piece of the picture (bottom part of body, tail, and feet) while you say the second syllable *key.* The child should physically move the picture pieces in some way (e.g., slide the pieces of the picture on the table, pick them up and place them on the table, or any physical involvement requiring touching the picture pieces simultaneously while hearing the sounds).

• Bounce a ball or jump a rope to the number of individual sounds or phonemes within one-syllable words (e.g., /s/, /u/, /n/—three bounces or jumps) or to the syllables in a multisyllable word *(el•e•va•tor* = four bounces or jumps).

In addition to any of Dr. Seuss's books, the following are examples of books that play with sounds, and help to build phonological awareness:

Brown, M.W. *Four Fur Feet.* New York: Hyperion Books for Children, 1989.

DeRegnier, B., E. Moore, M. White, and J. Carr. *Sing a Song of Popcorn.* New York: Scholastic, 1988.

Downes, Belinda. *A Stitch in Rhyme.* New York: Random House, 1996.

Galdone, P. *Henny Penny.* New York: Scholastic, 1986.

Guarino, D. *Is Your Mama a Llama?* New York: Scholastic, 1989.

Jonas, A. *Watch William Walk.* New York: Greenwillow Books, 1997.

Lear, Edward. *The Owl and the Pussy Cat.* New York: Clarion Books, 1987.

Martin, Jr., Bill. *The Happy Hippopotami.* New York: Holt, Rinehart & Winston, Inc., 1970.

Prelutsky, Jack. *Read-Aloud Rhymes for the Very Young.* New York: Alfred A. Knopf, 1986.

Ray, Karen. *Sleep Song.* New York: Orchard, 1995.

Shaw, Nancy. *Sheep on a Jeep.* Boston, MA: Houghton Mifflin Co., 1986.

Showers, P. *The Listening Walk.* New York: Harper Trophy, 1991.

Helping Your Child
Learn the Alphabet

One of the most important skills and concepts that emergent readers and writers must learn is knowledge of the alphabet at all levels. In addition to being able to recite the sequence of ABCs, children must learn the names and shapes of letters and recognize them in isolation (when shown one at a time in random order). They must acquire automatic association of the letter symbol to its matching sound. That is, when they see the letter *s*, they know it says */s/*. They need to identify correctly all upper-case (also called capital) and lower-case letters of the alphabet and their sounds, and be able to match them to each other. For example, if given plastic letters or magnetic letters *b, f, m, g, a,* and *B, F, M, G, A,* your child should put the matches together and then tell you, "*B* says */b/* like *boy* or *box*. *G* says */g/* like *girl* or *goat*." To read, we must be completely automatic in our ability to recognize a letter of the alphabet and say its sound. To write, we must first decide the *sound* to put to paper, and know with speed and automaticity which letter symbol represents that sound. Then we need to know how to *form* that letter symbol to write it from memory or looking at a model.

Mastery of the alphabet is *very complex* and *not an easy task*. All children typically enter kindergarten with alphabet knowledge and competency to some degree. Few have acquired full knowledge and mastery of the alphabet. An important part of kindergarten is practice so children have mastered the alphabet and can use it at an automatic level by the time they enter first grade.

In teaching the alphabet, it is important to give children many enjoyable experiences that are "hands-on" (not paper and pencil). Children of all ages learn best when something is taught in a way that is multisensory, that is, using as many senses as possible. When children have the opportunity not just to see or hear something, but also to hold it, use their hands and fingers to manipulate and *feel* it, then learning is facilitated.

You can purchase sets of upper-case and lower-case alphabet letters made from a variety of textures and materials (e.g., sponge letters, magnetic letters, plastic letters, felt letters, sandpaper letters). Your child will be interested in alphabet letters made of different colors and textures that he or she can pick up, touch, and manipulate. The most important and motivating letters for your child to learn how to identify first are the letters in his or her name. Some names begin with letters that aren't the common sound for that letter. For example, Charlotte begins with the letter C, but sounds like /sh/, not the common sound for C which is the sound heard in "cat" or "cup." If your child's name or others' in your family don't have the typical sound for a letter, in order not to confuse your child say: "Your name is spelled with one of the special sounds. It's different than most."

The Following Are Ways You Can Help Your Child Learn the Alphabet:

• Help your child learn how to sing the alphabet song in sequence of the alphabet letters.

• Watch television programming geared to early childhood (e.g., *Sesame Street*) that is motivational and helpful for children learning the alphabet.

• Look into appropriate computer software programs that may be motivating and engaging to youngsters learning the alphabet.

• Read ABC books frequently with your child. There are a number of beautiful alphabet books, including the following:

Azarian, Mary. *A Farmer's Alphabet*. Boston: David R. Godine, 1985.

Bender, R. *The A to Z Beastly Jamboree*. New York: Lodestar Books, 1996.

Gustafson, Scott. *Alphabet Soup: A Feast of Letters*. New York: Greenwich Workshop Press, 1994.

Hague, Kathleen. *Alphabears*. New York: Henry, Holt and Company, 1999.

Hoban, Tana. *A.B.See!* New York: Scholastic, Inc., 1984.

Kitamura, Satoshi. *From Acorn to Zoo and Everything in Between in Alphabetical Order*. New York: Scholastic, Inc., 1992.

Laidlaw, Ken. *The Amazing I Spy ABC*. New York: Dial Books, 1991.

Martin, Jr., Bill, and John Archambault. *Chicka Chicka Boom Boom*. New York: Simon & Schuster, 1989.

Nathan, Cheryl. *Bugs and Beasties ABC*. New York: CookKids Press, 1995.

Pallotta, Jerry. *The Icky Bug Alphabet Book*. New York: The Trumpet Club, 1986.

Sardegna, J. *K Is for Kiss Good Night: A Bedtime Alphabet*. New York: Picture Yearling, 1996.

Van Allsburg, Chris. *The Z Was Zapped*. Boston: Houghton Mifflin, 1998.

Wilbur, Richard. *The Disappearing Alphabet*. New York: Harcourt Brace, 1997.

• Make a collection of objects, such as small toys or those little things most of us uncover when digging through a junk drawer in the house. Collect a variety of objects that begin with the different letters of the alphabet. For example, for letter A you might find a plastic apple or rubber alligator. For *B* you may find a bandage or a small plastic toy—baby, bear, boat, or bathtub. For *C* you may find a small plastic cowboy, clock, cow, camera, or cookie; and so forth. As you find objects for each of the beginning letter sounds (toys or real things such as old, unused watch for *W,* keys for *K,* etc.) keep them together in a container or self-lock bag. These objects are perfect for learning sound association to the different letters. As your child is being introduced to a new letter of the alphabet in nursery school or kindergarten, help your child find and play with objects that begin with that sound. For example, if your child's class is focusing on the letter *T,* a great way for you to reinforce that learning is to have your child touch and play with objects that begin with the /t/ sound, as well as review the letter/sounds previously taught.

• Make a collection of pictures of everyday objects beginning with the different alphabet letters. Both the picture and object collection will be very useful in games and activities that will help your child learn. When your child has mastered the alphabet, you can donate the collection to your child's preschool or kindergarten.

• Using the collection of objects and pictures for each of the letters, have your child play games and do activities involving locating the letter that matches the beginning sound of the object/picture. Various containers (e.g., boxes, plastic tubs), each with a letter of the alphabet written on it, can be used. Your child sorts the objects, finding the proper container in which to place the corresponding object or picture.

• Play with charade-type games using action words that begin with the target sound. For example, to help remember the sound of *s* or /s/, you and your child can act out or pretend to /s/ sssneeze, /s/ sssnore, /s/ ssskip, /s/ sssswim, /s/ sssleep, and so forth.

• To help remember the letter/sound associations for the alphabet, it is always effective to use food. We remember a lot when we are able to use our *sense of taste.* For example, to help remember the sound of *G,* point out that *g* makes the sound of /g/ *grapes* and *granola.* If trying to remember the sound of *B,* help your child associate the letter *b* with /b/ *bagels,* /b/ *brownies,* /b/ *bananas,* /b/ *bologna,* /b/ *bread and butter.*

• Practice forming the letters of the alphabet with your child using tactile strategies involving the *sense of touch.* When they *feel* the formation of the letter, children recall the visual image as well as the movements required in actually writing the letter. It is also important to remember that young children first develop and learn best through large muscle movements (moving their full arm) before they become proficient with small hand and finger movements. Try the following techniques when helping your child learn how to form alphabet letters correctly:

— Write letters in the air moving the arm in large strokes. You may need to guide your child by gently holding his or her wrist as you go through the motions of forming the letter and saying its name and/or sound.

— Write letters on your child's back with your fingers and let him or her guess the letter you are making.

— Help your child to write letters with large strokes using two fingers like the index and middle fingers on the carpet. Guide your child's hand as you form the letter by placing your hand gently over your child's.

— Help your child paint the letters using a paint brush. Use an easel if you have one.

— Help your child practice writing letters with a damp sponge on a chalkboard, or a paint brush that has only water (not paint) on it.

— Help your child practice writing alphabet letters on a Magna Doodle.™

— Help your child write letters in a sandbox using a stick or your child's fingers.

— Use frosting or pudding on a paper plate or waxed paper to practice writing letters with a finger.

— Write letters on a dry-erase board with colored dry-erase pens. Then have your child trace over in the same formation using his or her finger (erasing the letter while doing so).

— Help your child form letters using clay or Play-Doh.™

— Help your child form letters using Wikki-Sticks™ (produced by Omnicor, Inc., Phoenix, AZ: 1-800-869-4554).

— Help your child write letters in glue or liquid starch on pieces of cardboard. Then sprinkle any powdery material (glitter, colored sand) or cover with yarn, dry macaroni, sequins, etc., to create textured, three-dimensional letters. The act of tracing with the fingers on a texture helps make a sensory imprint on the brain that helps build your child's memory for the letter formation.

You can help your child make his or her own ABC book. Use a new page for each letter of the alphabet and help locate pictures from magazines that begin with the sound for the letter on the page. You may wish to use the same letters being taught in your child's preschool or kindergarten class. Typically, letters are introduced not in alphabetical order but by the frequency of that letter in word use. For example, the letters *m, s,* and *t* are more common and frequently found in words than the letters *q* and *z,* so they are generally taught first. When making the alphabet book, help your child find and choose pictures that begin with the common beginning *sound* for the letter. The spelling of the word is not important, nor is it the focus. So a picture of a shoe would not be a good choice for the *S* page, because its beginning sound is */sh/,* not */s/.* You want the page to be filled with the common sound for *s,* which is the sound you hear in *sun, seal,* and *snake.*

There are numerous exciting and motivating ABC games and activities that your young child will love in the book *Alphabet Learning Center Activities Kit* (N. Fetzer and S. Rief). Directions or recipes for making many home or school learning center activities are provided. Activities include: ABC Pocket Books, ABC Button Up, ABC Velcro Match, ABC Sock Clothesline, ABC Apron, ABC Tablecloth, Alphabet Fishing, ABC Jewelry Boxes, ABC Mystery Can, ABC Silverware, ABC Sound Sticks, ABC Sound Puzzles, ABC Egg Twist, and ABC Clothespins.

Many of the tactile strategies for practicing the formation of alphabet letters in a variety of ways are demonstrated in the video *How to Help Your Child Succeed in School.* (See the back of this book for ordering information on these resources.)

What Research Says About Preventing Reading Difficulties

Evidence based on thirty years of research investigating how children learn to read, why some children struggle in learning how to read, and what can be done to prevent reading difficulties has become available. This information should guide decisions regarding reading instruction and practices.

One of the main sources of the research information is the National Institute of Child Health and Human Development (NICHD), National Institutes of Health. The NICHD has supported scientific research continuously since 1965 to understand normal reading development and reading difficulties. The NICHD developed a research network consisting of forty-one research sites in North America (and other parts of the world) that conducted numerous studies on thousands of children, many over a period of years. The findings from this wealth of research were presented as testimony by G. Reid Lyon, Ph.D., Chief of the Child Development and Behavior Branch of the NICHD, National Institutes of Health, to the Committee on Labor and Human Resources, U.S. Senate, in 1998.

In addition, the Committee on the Prevention of Reading Difficulties in Young Children, National Research Council, provided research findings. This committee was charged by the National Academy of Sciences with conducting a study of the effectiveness of interventions for young children who are at risk of reading difficulties.

The committee reviewed research on normal reading development and instruction; on risk factors useful in identifying groups and individuals at risk of reading failure; and on prevention, intervention, and instructional approaches to ensuring optimal reading outcomes. The committee's results are presented in *Preventing Reading Difficulties in Young Children,* edited by Catherine E. Snow, Susan M. Burns, and Peg Griffin (Washington, D.C.: National Academy Press, 1998).

The following facts are based on the aforementioned research (if you want more information on the studies, refer to the bibliography at the end of this section):

• NICHD studies show that one child in five will experience significant difficulty learning to read well enough to utilize reading for education and for enjoyment. Other studies show higher figures (e.g., 30 to 40 percent of children will have significant difficulty learning to read).

• Reading difficulties persist. Longitudinal studies indicate that of children who are reading disabled in the third grade, approximately 70 percent remain disabled at the end of high school.

• Failure to read proficiently is the most likely reason that children drop out of school, are retained, or are referred to special education.

• Approximately 50 percent of reading difficulties can be prevented if students are provided effective language development in preschool and kindergarten and effective reading instruction in the primary grades.

• There is a strong association between a child's ability to read and his or her ability to segment words into phonemes (hear and separate a spoken word into its individual sounds, such as *pig* as /p/ /i/ /g/.

• Phonemic awareness skills assessed in kindergarten and first grade (with tasks that take only fifteen minutes to administer) can predict with high accuracy those children who will have difficulty learning to read.

- Kindergarten children's phonemic awareness can predict their levels of reading and spelling achievement even years later. It is a more powerful predictor of reading progress than I.Q. scores.

- Children who receive explicit instruction in phonemic awareness and phonological awareness show greater gains in reading skills than those children without this instruction.

- We must explicitly teach the alphabetic code, sound spellings, and phonemic awareness in order to prevent reading difficulties. By providing this explicit instruction, we may prevent many children from the need of entering special education programs. (As many as 80 percent of referrals to special education involve reading difficulties.)

- Learning letter/sound correspondence (necessary for reading and spelling) requires an awareness that spoken language can be analyzed as strings of separate words. These words are comprised of sequences of syllables; and syllables are made up of smaller units of sounds (phonemes).

- The most frequent characteristic observed among children and adults with reading disabilities is a slow, labored approach to decoding or "sounding out" unknown or unfamiliar words and frequent misidentification of familiar words.

- Some types of reading disability appear to have a genetic cause, with deficits in phonemic awareness being the greatest hereditary factor.

- The vast majority of students with reading difficulties can learn to read when given intensive instruction using research-validated practices.

- First-grade decoding ability predicts 80 to 90 percent of reading comprehension in second and third grades and nearly 40 percent of reading comprehension by ninth grade.

- Fluency is highly correlated with reading comprehension. When children read fluently, they can use their language skills, reasoning skills, and background knowledge to comprehend text. In contrast, those who have inadequate reading fluency struggle with the text, which diminishes their ability to comprehend.

• Effective prevention and early intervention programs can increase the reading skills of 85 to 90 percent of poor readers to average levels.

• Most children with severe reading difficulty have substantial weakness in auditory-related skills (e.g., phonemic awareness) and in associating those sounds with the printed letter (sound/symbol relationships).

• Adequate initial reading instruction requires that children:
   —use reading to obtain meaning from print
   —have frequent and intensive opportunities to read
   —are exposed to frequent, regular spelling/sound relationships
   —learn about the nature of the alphabetic writing system
   —understand the structure of spoken words

• The three main obstacles on the journey to skilled reading:
   —difficulty understanding and using the alphabetic principle (the idea that written spellings systematically represent spoken words)
   —failure to transfer the comprehension skills of spoken language to reading and to acquire new strategies that may be needed for reading
   —absence or loss of an initial motivation to read, or failure to develop a mature appreciation of the rewards of reading (See Catherine Snow et al., *Preventing Reading Difficulties in Young Children,* National Research Council, Washington, D.C.: National Academy Press, 1998.)

• "In the initial stages of reading development, learning phoneme awareness and phonics skills and practicing these skills with texts is critical. Children must also acquire fluency and automaticity in decoding and word recognition. Consider that a reader has only so much attention and memory capacity. If beginning readers read the words in a laborious, inefficient manner, they cannot remember what they read, much less relate the ideas to their background knowledge. Thus, the ultimate goal of reading instruction for children to understand and enjoy what they read may not be achieved." (See G. Reid Lyon, "Why reading is not a natural process," *LDA Newsbriefs,* Jan./Feb. 2000, **www.ldonline.org/ld-in-depth/reading/why-reading-is-not.html**).

• Children who are most at risk for reading failure enter kindergarten limited in their awareness of sound structure and language pattern, phonemic sensitivity, letter knowledge, and the purposes of reading; and they have had little exposure to books and print.

• "Kindergarten instruction should be designed to provide practice with the sound structure of words, the recognition and production of letters, knowledge about print concepts, and familiarity with the basic purposes and mechanisms of reading and writing." (See Catherine Snow et al., *Preventing Reading Difficulties in Young Children,* National Research Council, Washington, D.C.: National Academy Press, 1998.)

The research shows that the parents' role is very important in helping to prevent reading difficulties in children. According to the research, even a brief amount of time daily with your child sitting on your lap or close to you as you read a picture book together makes a significant difference in your child's acquisition of basic reading skills. Singing songs, reading rhyming books, and playing games that focus on sounds and syllables within words are vital ways you can help your child develop the prerequisite skills for being a reader. Help your child to acquire the awareness of letters and their corresponding sounds (e.g., through looking together at ABC books, playing games such as listening for words that begin with a certain sound, and so forth). These skills are critical to your child's development. Parents and teachers need to work together to make sure each child acquires these skills.

Bibliography

Adams, M. J. *Beginning to Read: Thinking and Learning About Print* (1990). Cambridge, MA: MIT Press.

The California Reading Initiative and Special Education in California—Critical Ideas Focusing on Meaningful Reform (1999), developed by the Special Education Reading Task Force, the California Department of Education, and the California State Board of Education. Sacramento, CA: California Department of Education. See the full document at www.cde.ca.gov/spbranch/sed/resources.htm.

Fletcher, J. M., and G. R. Lyon (1998). "Reading: A Research Based Approach," in *What's Gone Wrong in America's Classrooms.* Edited by W. Evers. Stanford, CA: Hoover Institution Press, Stanford University.

Foorman B. R., D. J. Francis, J. M. Fletcher, C. Schatschneider, and P. Mehta (1998). "The role of instruction in learning to read: Preventing reading failure in at-risk children." *Journal of Educational Psychology,* 90, 115.

Good, R. H., D. C. Simmons, and S. B. Smith (1998). "Effective academic intervention in the United States: Evaluating and enhancing the acquisition of early reading skills." *School Psychology Review,* 27 (1), 45–56.

Honig, B. (1999). "Reading the Right Way," *CORE Reading Research Anthology.* Novato, CA: Arena Press, Consortium on Reading Excellence, Inc.

Kavale, K. A., and J. H. Reese (1992). "The character of learning disabilities: An Iowa profile." *Learning Disabilities Quarterly,* 15 (2), 74–94.

Liberman, A. M. (1992). "The Relation of Speech to Reading and Writing," in *Orthography, Phonology, Morphology, and Meaning.* Edited by R. Frost and L. Katz. Amsterdam: Elsevier Science Publishers B.V.

Liberman, I. Y., D. Shankweiler, and A. M. Liberman (1989). "The Alphabetic Principle and Learning to Read," in *Phonology and Reading Disability; Solving the Reading Puzzle.* Edited by D. P. Shankweiler and I. Y. Liberman, IARLD Monograph Series. Ann Arbor: University of Michigan Press.

Lyon, G. R. (1998). "Overview of Reading and Literacy Initiatives," testimony provided to the Committee on Labor and Human Resources, U.S. Senate. Bethesda, MD: National Institute of Child Health and Human Development.

———— (1998). "Why reading is not a natural process," *Educational Leadership,* 55 (6), 14–18. Also found in *LDA Newsbriefs,* Learning Disabilities Association of America, LD Online Reading (2000), **www.ldonline.org/ld_indepth/reading/reading.html**.

———— (1999). "The NICHD Research Program in Reading Development, Reading Disorders and Reading Instruction: A Summary of Research Findings," publication from *Keys to Successful Learning: A National Summit on Research in Learning Disabilities.* New York: The National Center for Learning Disabilities.

Lyon, G. R., and L. C. Moats (1997). "Critical conceptual and methodological considerations in reading intervention research." *Journal of Learning Disabilities,* 30, 578–588.

Simmons, D. C. (editor) and E. J. Kamelenui (1998). *What Reading Research Tells Us About Children with Diverse Learning Needs: Bases and Basics.* Mahwah, NJ: Lawrence Erlbaum Associates, Inc.

Slavin, R., N. Karweit, and B. Wasik (1993). "Preventing early school failure: What works?" *Educational Leadership,* 50 (4), 10–17.

Snow, C. E., M. S. Burns, and P. Griffin, Editors (1998). *Preventing Reading Difficulties in Young Children,* National Research Council. Washington, DC: National Academy Press.

Torgesen, J. K. (1998). "Catch them before they fall." *American Educator,* 22 (1 and 2), 32–39.

What to Expect
in the Emergent
and Beginning Levels
of Reading Development

Most children enter kindergarten with some rudimentary knowledge about reading and written language. They may know enough about reading from their experience and the examples they have seen to pick up books and pretend to read or to imitate the behaviors of a reader. At the emergent level of reading development, children begin to grasp a number of critical concepts and skills. They start acquiring the awareness of print—what it means and how it works. They develop in their understanding of the alphabetic principle—that those marks on a page are symbols representing sounds that can go together (in an infinite number of ways or combinations) to represent the different words we speak. Children at this emergent stage begin to recognize more of those letters of the alphabet with automaticity, along with their corresponding sound association. They gain in their phonemic and phonological awareness and in their competence in general book-handling skills. Emergent readers begin to understand and utilize an ever-increasing number of reading strategies and behaviors in their attempt to become independent readers.

Of course, reading development in every child will be different. Each child will vary in his or her rate of skill acquisition. Some children enter kindergarten already reading or on the verge of doing so. Other children will be at this stage a few months into the kindergarten year, or later. For those not developmentally ready, it will take much longer. This is normal and to be expected. Kindergarten teachers should be prepared for the developmental range of students and provide extra support and assistance to those children who need it, as well as challenging and motivating more advanced readers.

The following are some of the skills and behaviors that are part of any kindergarten curriculum. Teachers must teach these skills so students are able to meet performance standards by the end of the kindergarten year.

Alphabet

- Recites sequentially
- Recognizes and names upper-case and lower-case letters
- Matches upper-case to lower-case letters
- Shows rapid, automatic recognition of and production of most common sound associated with each letter
- Matches letters and sounds
- Locates letters in the environment and within printed words

Getting Meaning from Print

- Is aware that print carries meaning
- Is aware that text matches the spoken, oral language, and purpose is communication of message
- Can retell simple stories, getting main events in proper sequence
- Turns pages to find out what happens next
- Makes predictions while reading
- Demonstrates comprehension of stories read to him or her by responding to some questions (e.g., regarding the content, main idea, characters, events, and outcome)
- Makes connections between characters, events, and situations in books to those in his or her life
- Uses background knowledge and prior experience to get meaning and make connections with text

- When hearing texts that have been read several times and are familiar, can repeat some words, phrases, or verse with proper intonation
- When hearing texts that have been read several times and are familiar, can fill in missing words, phrases, verses, or endings, when the reader pauses and prompts the child to do so

Concepts of Print and Book-Handling Skills

- Understands that printed words are made up of specific combinations and sequences of letters that represent their spoken sounds
- Understands one-to-one correspondence of printed words and spoken words
- Differentiates first and last letters of words
- Tracks and points to words being read, matching spoken word to printed word
- Identifies and understands basic punctuation (e.g., periods, question marks)
- Differentiates between capital and lower-case letters and knows sentences and names begin with capital or upper-case letters
- Holds book correctly
- Recognizes front and back of book
- Recognizes the title page
- Knows author's and illustrator's roles
- Knows where to begin reading, and in what direction
- Knows directionality of English text going from left to right and from top to bottom
- Turns pages at the right time, in the right direction
- Understands return sweep at end of line to the beginning of the next line
- Recognizes where words are and spaces between
- Understands that print contains the message

- Understands that illustrations are related to the text
- Recognizes that both illustrations and text carry meaning and information

Phonemic and Phonological Awareness

- Understands that words are made up of a sequence of separate distinct sounds/phonemes
- Differentiates between sounds; is able to hear and recognize the subtle differences of similar-sounding words (e.g., *hid/head*)
- Recognizes and identifies rhyming words
- Recognizes words that have the same beginning sounds
- Recognizes words that have the same ending sounds

Pleasure and Purpose in Reading

- Looks at books for pleasure
- Pays attention when being read to
- Requests that books be read to him or her
- Shows interest and enjoyment in stories and illustrations
- Has favorite books and stories and asks to have them read frequently
- Attempts to imitate or mimic reading independently (e.g., "reads" a book to younger sibling, stuffed animal, or doll)
- Picks out letters and words known in text and in the environment
- Memorizes some simple books or parts of them
- Knows that information and answers to questions can be found in different texts (e.g., newspapers, magazines, labels, books, recipes, directions that accompany games, etc.)
- Has interest in books or texts of different genres (e.g., folk tales, predictable pattern books, nursery rhymes, poetry, informational concept books)

Beginning Word Recognition and Decoding

- Recognizes own name and an increasing number of words commonly found in the environment that are familiar to the child
- Recognizes and reads with automaticity some common, high-frequency words that are not to be sounded out but identified by sight (e.g., *the, said, from)*
- Tries reading words from labels, road signs, and other environmental print
- Uses whatever knowledge child has of letter/sound association and phonics for attempting to "sound out" unknown words (e.g., the beginning sound of the word only, the beginning and ending sounds of the word, the initial blend or consonant digraph—*sp, bl, sh, ch,* and so forth)
- Attempts to blend phonemes sequentially to decode unknown words
- Uses beginning knowledge of word patterns to figure out unfamiliar words (e.g., recognition of onset and rime and word families */-at/, /-ad/, /-ip/, /-op/, /-ock/*). For example, "I know *it* and *sit;* so that word must be *fit."*
- Uses beginning knowledge of word parts such as inflectional endings (e.g., *-ing, -s, -ed*) to figure out unknown words.

In addition, emergent- and beginning-level readers are taught how to use multiple strategies to figure out unfamiliar words and get meaning from text. Through modeling and guiding by the teacher or other adults and proficient readers, the child learns the following:

- To monitor his or her own reading and try self-correcting if words read don't look right, sound right, or make sense
- To attempt a few different strategies that focus on the graphophonics clues (or what is known about the letters/sounds within the word), the structural clues (the child's knowledge of oral language—what sounds right when we talk), the context clues, meaning of words, picture clues, or other information on the page that helps in determining if what is being read makes sense

As children develop the skills to begin reading some simple books during the emergent-level stage, the initial books read typically have the following features:

1. The print is large and well spaced, making it easy to match word by word, and point to each word with a finger.
2. There is a very simple story line or single concept/idea that the child can easily relate to from his or her own experience.
3. There is a direct match between the words and the illustrations shown.
4. The vocabulary is familiar to the child.
5. Sentences have very simple grammatical structure and are short in length.
6. There are, at most, two sentences on a page, and the sentences often follow a pattern throughout the text (e.g., one or two word changes within a repeating sentence frame).

It is important that as soon as children know enough letters to form some words, they are given practice doing so. For example, once children know the letter/sound association for *m, t, r, a, s,* they are able to start combining those letters to read real words *at, mat, rat, sat, am, Sam, ram.* It is also important that once they have some word recognition (e.g., *the, I, am, to*) and strategies to begin trying to read very simple text, they are given books that allow them to use their skills. The more children are engaged in practicing being a reader, the sooner they will become one. They will need to continue to be read to daily, but they also need to try reading to themselves and to you.

As children's reading development advances throughout the kindergarten year and beyond, books selected for them to read independently or with minimal support will begin to have more sentences or print on the pages. Less information will be gleaned from the illustrations and much more from the print. Sentence structure will become more complex and varied. The books will begin to have a more involved or sophisticated story line.

Additional Help This Book Offers

For more strategies for helping your child in the emerging- and beginning-level stages of reading, see the following sections: "What Good Readers Do—Positive Reading Behaviors," "How to Ask Questions That Guide Your Child in Developing Good Reading Strategies and Thinking Skills," "Getting Them Off to a Good Start: Strategies for Developing Emergent and Beginning Reading Skills," "Building Vocabulary and Comprehension Skills," "Beginning Phonics, Word Recognition, and Word Study Skills," and "The Importance of Read-Alouds and Shared Reading: Strategies for Reading *to* and *with* Your Child."

Getting Them Off to a Good Start: Strategies for Developing Emergent and Beginning Reading Skills

The early years of your child's life are critical in establishing the foundation for reading. The following strategies will help you create an environment that encourages reading and writing and communicates the value of the written word.

• Get your child his or her own library card and visit the library often. Ask the librarian to recommend books that are popular at your child's age level and for titles of award-winning (e.g., Caldecott Medal and Newbery Medal) books.

• Obtain the schedule of events at the local library and children's books stores. There are often special events such as puppet shows and storytellers, as well as story hours or times when books are read to children.

• Fill your home with books and keep your child's books in reachable, accessible locations, such as plastic bins on wheels, boxes and other containers, a couple of low bookshelves or drawers. Keep books and children's magazines in different locations of the house, including your child's room, in the family room or den, in a basket in the bathroom.

• Participate whenever possible in different storytelling and other literacy activities for children in your community.

- Become a regular patron of your local children's books store. The owners and employees of children's books stores are often excellent resources. They are frequently able to recommend popular titles and can steer you in the right direction when you are looking for good, appropriate books for your child.

- Buy books often. Instead of gifts and rewards of toys, purchase books for your child and others. Books can be purchased at an inexpensive price through school book clubs; garage or yard sales; thrift shops; used book sales at libraries, schools, and so forth. It is often worth rummaging through those cartons of used books for great finds that may cost as low as a dime or quarter! Read these books to your children.

- Limit the time your child spends in front of the TV or playing video games. Instead, engage more in singing, nursery and action rhymes, looking through books and magazines, talking and playing games involving language, reading and writing together, and taking your child places that will build his or her knowledge base, vocabulary, and understanding of the world (e.g., parks, nature walks, museums, the zoo).

- Play games involving looking for alphabet letters in the environment (on signs, on labels, in the newspaper or magazine).

- Play a variety of games, such as Bingo or Go Fish, that utilize the letters or simple words your child knows (or is in the process of learning). See the section "Developmentally Appropriate Games, Books, Songs, Manipulatives, and Other Activities/Resources."

- Purchase alphabet letters made of different materials and textures and use them with your child to write words and play games (for example, plastic alphabet letters with magnets on the back, sponge letters, cardboard letters, felt letters, foam rubber letters, sandpaper letters, alphabet stamps and stickers, and so forth). You can even find cookies, cereal, and pasta in the shapes of alphabet letters!

- Encourage your child to read any words he or she recognizes in the environment (e.g., words on a billboard, traffic signs, names of stores, words on boxes of products around the house).

• Have your child help you read directions for how to make or do something (e.g., recipes, a new game).

• Write your child very simple, special messages and place them under pillows, in lunchboxes, in jacket pockets, inside a glove or mitten, or posted on mirrors or walls.

Additional Help This Book Offers

See the many fun activities that promote learning the alphabet, playing with words and language, prerequisite skills to reading (e.g., visual and auditory processing activities) found in other sections of this book, including "Helping Your Child Learn the Alphabet," "Language and Literacy: The Building Blocks of School Success," "Create a Home Environment That Encourages Success," "Playing with Sounds and Language," "Children with Learning Disabilities, Attention Deficit Disorders, and Other Special Needs" (the information section on auditory and visual processing skills/activities), and "Strategies for Building Fine Motor and Prewriting/Writing Skills."

The most important way to get your child off to a good start in reading and to help in the development of positive reading behaviors is to read to and with your child. The educational jargon for these reading activities is *read-aloud* and *shared reading.* Any preschool, kindergarten, or elementary classroom includes these two components in its literacy curriculum. See the section "The Importance of Read-Alouds and Shared Reading: Strategies for Reading *to* and *with* Your Child."

There are other recommended strategies and activities for helping your child develop emergent- and beginning-level reading skills. See the sections "What Good Readers Do: Positive Reading Behaviors," "Building Vocabulary and Comprehension Skills," "How to Ask Questions That Guide Your Child in Developing Good Reading Strategies and Thinking Skills," and "Beginning Phonics, Word Recognition, and Word Study Skills."

What Good Readers Do— Positive Reading Behaviors

There are a number of specific behaviors and competencies of good readers that we want to develop in children. Good readers are skilled at efficiently applying decoding strategies to figure out unknown words in print. They have the phonics and word recognition skills they need so they don't have to struggle to decipher many of the words of text. Therefore, they can read with speed and fluency and focus their attention on the meaning of what they read rather than the mechanics of doing so. See the section "What the Research Says about Preventing Reading Difficulties."

In addition, good readers appreciate and explore different aspects of words and language. They typically have knowledge of word meanings, concepts, and language comprehension based on their prior knowledge, exposure, and experiences. They read and reread books frequently and get pleasure from books and other printed material. Of course, the more they read, the more proficient they become in vocabulary, word knowledge, and comprehension skills.

More important, skilled and proficient readers are good *comprehenders*. They know that the purpose of reading is to get meaning from the print, and they use multiple strategies to do so. Good readers monitor their own comprehension. If something doesn't make sense as they are reading, or if they make an error that affects their ability to understand the text, they will try to self-correct the error. For example, they may return to the beginning of the line, sentence, or previous few words and reread. They may first read to the end of the line, skipping over the unknown word(s), and use various strategies and cueing systems to go back and determine what word(s) would make sense. *Graphophonic* cues involve looking carefully at the printed unknown word and using knowledge of letters/letter combinations and their corresponding sounds to help figure out what the unknown word may be. *Syntax* cues involve listening carefully to the words read and determining if they sound right and if they sound like the way we would speak—make sense grammatically and follow our English rules of sentence structure. *Semantic* cues involve listening and looking for meaning—if the word makes sense the way it is being used; if it meshes with or correlates with other information (e.g., the illustration, the reader's own background knowledge).

Actively thinking about the words they read and their message, and making guesses or predictions while reading about what may happen next, is another characteristic of skilled readers. As they read, they are either confirming their predictions or adjusting and revising them as they progress through the text. They are also thinking about any connections, associations, or similarities to their own life and experiences. Good readers/comprehenders are able to visualize as they read or hear the words. They can typically make a mental picture and see the picture and actions in their mind's eye. Good readers/thinkers can understand and identify the main idea of the text. With literature, they understand basic story structure—characters, setting, the basic plot including problems and solution, and the sequence of events (beginning, middle, and end). With informational or expository text, such as science or social studies books or news articles, they can identify the main ideas and supporting details. These readers have confidence in their abilities. They are willing to take risks and engage in many kinds of reading and literacy experiences. Because they have had success as independent readers, they are, therefore, more motivated to read.

Your child will receive instruction in all of these important reading behaviors, strategies, and skills in school and will continue developing and advancing in these skills throughout the grades. However, the reading skills a child learns in the primary grades are the most important in determining how good a reader the child will be. Research shows that children who are poor readers in the third grade will likely always be poor readers. We must start every child on the right path toward literacy and intervene early if a child is having problems learning to read. Parents and teachers need to work together to ensure that every child becomes a skilled reader.

Additional Help This Book Offers

There is much that you can do during the preschool/kindergarten years to help. Now is the time to build your child's literacy foundation. Give your child the experiences he or she needs in order to become a competent and confident independent reader. See sections "Getting Them Off to a Good Start: Strategies for Developing Emergent and Beginning Reading Skills," "How to Ask Questions that Guide Your Child in Developing Good Reading Strategies and Thinking Skills," "What the Research Says about Preventing Reading Difficulties," "Kindergarten Performance Standards," "What to Expect in the Emergent and Beginning Levels of Reading Development," "The Importance of Read-Alouds and Shared Reading: Strategies for Reading *to* and *with* Your Child," "Building Vocabulary and Comprehension Skills," and "Beginning Phonics, Word Recognition, and Word Study Skills."

The Importance of Read-Alouds and Shared Reading: Strategies for Reading *to* and *with* Your Child

The most effective way to plant the seeds of literacy and help children grow into competent readers and writers is through the process of reading to and with them every day. An abundance of research shows that children who have stronger literacy skills have had more exposure to language and literacy experiences.

It is never too early to start reading to your child. Even infants and toddlers benefit from listening to the stimulating language of books, especially while being held, cuddled, or sitting on a loved one's lap. As early and frequently as possible, give your child the experience of associating reading with enjoyment and pleasure. There are many skills and concepts your child acquires through the process of sitting close to the reader, observing and looking at the print and illustrations, and listening to the book or story being read. This includes:

- Print awareness and understanding that the marks on the page separated by spaces represent the words we speak
- Awareness that good readers can read or say those words fluently and with a voice that sounds like we talk—that flows and is smooth (not choppy) and phrased (not word by word)
- Awareness that the words on the page carry meaning and that we need to listen to them and think about the words to get the meaning
- Directionality in that we read in English from left to right, and from top to bottom

- Many new vocabulary words that are taught through the context of phrases/sentences and illustrations of the story
- Phonological awareness and other auditory processing skills—tuning into the sounds of language
- Book language that is often different from the language we use in everyday speech and communication—for example, more complex and varied sentence structure and vocabulary usage
- Attention and listening comprehension skills
- Visual processing skills such as attention to detail in illustrations, pointing out and recognizing letters/words
- Awareness of different genres and styles of writing
- Awareness and understanding story format or story grammar and the common elements that can be found in stories (e.g., characters, setting, problem[s], sequence of events leading to resolution of problem[s] with beginning, middle, and end)
- Thinking skills such as predicting, confirming predictions, or adjusting and revising them, making connections and associations, visualizing, and so forth
- Knowledge and concept building

There is much to be gained when children are read to and when they have the chance to interact with an adult or other reader model while engaged with an interesting and exciting book. This has been discussed in many of the other sections of this book. The two main techniques for reading to and with children are referred to as the read-aloud and shared reading.

What Do These Techniques Look Like in the Classroom?

READ-ALOUD

During the read-aloud portion of the classroom day, children are typically seated on a carpet close to the teacher as he or she reads to them from a book. The teacher reads orally with fluency, expression, and enthusiasm and takes the time to show all of the students the pictures before turning the page. The teacher has first introduced the book, pointed out the author and illustrator, and has engaged the students prior to reading in some way—asking a speculative question, having children guess or predict what the story is about, telling something that the book will be about, drawing upon a connection to the students' previous experience and background knowledge.

During the reading, the teacher stops from time to time to ask the children to predict what will happen next or to express how they think a character is feeling at the time, and so forth. The teacher may model some effective comprehension strategies that will help children become more strategic, engaged readers. For example, the teacher may think or ponder out loud (e.g., "I wonder what is inside that box . . . I bet James is very excited now.").

The vocabulary and reading level of books chosen for reading aloud are at a challenging level for the children. The children can't yet read them on their own. When necessary, the teacher stops and talks about some word meanings, clarifies vocabulary/rephrases, explains some aspects of the story that may be confusing, and asks a few questions to make sure the children are comprehending the text. The teacher also guides students through discussion of the story grammar elements such as the characters, setting, problems encountered in the plot or story line, and the solution or outcome.

The teacher initiates discussion and follow-up activities of some sort about the book after reading it. Generally, the teacher tries to find books to read aloud that relate in some way to concepts or themes being taught in class, and to look for new books that the children are unfamiliar with. Of course, the teacher also finds time to reread the children's favorite stories and books. However, exposing children to the new language and concepts to be learned through reading of unfamiliar books and stories is a valuable feature of the read-aloud. The read-aloud is also the perfect vehicle for teaching the thinking skills so critical to becoming a reader.

SHARED READING

During a shared reading, the teacher typically sits or stands next to a chart stand that is holding a large chart with words of poems, verses, chants, songs, or rhymes printed in large, neat letters. The teacher may also sit or stand next to a "Big Book," which is propped up or supported on some kind of stand or rack. The children are clustered around so they can easily view the words of the chart or Big Book as the teacher points to them (often with a pointer or stick of some kind). If a Big Book is used, the story line is simple. Generally it contains predictable text or a repeating pattern that is easy for young children to follow. Some of the same kind of talking and questioning—prior, during, and after the reading—may occur during shared reading as takes place during the read-aloud.

One of the main goals of shared reading is to engage all of the children in practicing what it's like to be a proficient reader. The text chosen becomes familiar to the children as they hear it over and over again from one day or week to the next. As the teacher models how to read with fluency and intonation while simultaneously pointing to the words as they are spoken, the children begin to learn the conventions of print and identify some common words. The children are encouraged to read along with the teacher, joining in as they are able to do so. There are many techniques that can be used to have fun and learn through shared reading. Examples include reciting the refrains, providing the missing word when the teacher pauses (such as the last word in rhyming lines), echoing back a line after the teacher reads it, reading together in unison, and alternating reading or taking turns.

The shared reading is a perfect opportunity for the teacher not only to model and have children practice positive reading behaviors, but to guide the children in attending to certain parts of the text, pointing out and reinforcing certain skills. For example, children may be asked to come up to the chart or Big Book and locate certain letters/sounds or words (e.g., all the words *to* on the page, all the words that begin with the letter *s* or that have the /b/ sound at the beginning). The teacher may point out the "talking marks" or quotation marks used or have children locate the words with capital letters and tell why they are capitalized. The teacher may also point out and model the process of using different cueing strategies when reading unfamiliar words.

Strategies for Reading *to* and *with* Your Child

As parents, you can do some of the same strategies with your child that teachers use during read-aloud and shared-reading instruction with students:

- Make it a part of the daily and nightly routine to read to or with your child—at least one book every day. Make reading together an important time of the day or evening, without being hassled and rushed. The special routine of bedtime stories should be established early and followed consistently.

- Read together while snuggling on a big chair, couch, or in bed, or with your child seated on your lap. Make sure you are both comfortable and that your child can easily see the pages of the book and touch the pictures and the print.

- Get everyone in the family involved in reading to your preschooler/kindergartner—grandparents, siblings, baby sitters.

- Ask in your library or local book stores for recommended titles of books for reading aloud to your young child. Choose books together with your child. There are wordless books in which you can engage your youngster in making up and telling the story based upon the pictures only. There are folk and fairy tales of different versions; nursery rhymes and songs; alphabet, counting, and other concept books; and so forth. There are thousands of wonderful choices of picture and story books that will delight your child and that you can enjoy together. With young children don't choose chapter books or anything lengthy that can't be read comfortably in one sitting. Children of this age level don't have the attention span or appreciation for those kinds of books.

- If your family's primary language is other than English, read books to your child in your native language. Books in many languages are available through your public library.

- Keep children's books accessible and easy to reach, and read together in different locations of the house. Also, keep daily reading in mind when on excursions, errands, or trips out of the home. Keep books for your child handy (e.g., in the trunk or glove compartment of your car).

• Take the time to read through the book yourself before reading it to your child. This way you are already familiar with the story line and some of the points you may want to call attention to when reading together. You might also choose to be more dramatic in your reading (e.g., taking on the voices of certain characters for greater interest). Prereading also alerts you to any challenging vocabulary you may want to paraphrase or explain when reading.

• Before reading the book, look together at the cover, read the title, and read the author's/illustrator's name(s). You may want to say something briefly about what the book is about (e.g., a little girl, Lisa, who is looking for her lost kitten). You may want to say something about where the story takes place (e.g., in the city, on a farm) or some other brief and basic information. Have your child walk through the pictures quickly—at least the first pages of pictures— and talk about some of them. Ask a question to engage your child in talking about the book (e.g., "What is the kitten doing here?" "Do you think Lisa is going to find her kitten?").

• Read the book with expression and enthusiasm. Pause while reading to talk with your child during the reading. Do so by asking a few questions periodically (e.g., "Where do you think Whiskers is going?" "Oh, look at Lisa's face. How do you think she feels?" "What would you do?" "Do you know what that word ____ means?"). Take the time to let your child talk about something he or she wants to point out or say during the reading—especially regarding the illustrations, predictions, and so forth.

• Make comments and think aloud while you read, such as "I'm getting worried. I wonder what Whiskers is going to do." "Oh, you guessed right, Whiskers is hiding behind the box."

• Pause to talk during the reading, but not to the extent that your child will lose track of the flow or sense of the story or feel less excited about the reading.

• Let your child turn the pages of the book you are reading. This gives him or her firsthand experience in handling a book.

- Point under the words with your finger and glide your finger along as you read with fluency. Your child will notice that we read sentences from left to right, and that sentences are composed of individual words.

- If there is a word your child knows how to read, you may ask your child to read that word when you come to it.

- At times you may wish to point out words with certain beginning letters/sounds or your child may want to do so.

- Books that have rhymes, repetitive verse, or refrains are perfect for having your child join in and say those words or phrases along with you. Also, with books your child knows well, stop or pause for certain words and let your child fill in the missing word. Especially with text that rhymes, pause at the end and let your child supply the word that completes the rhyming line.

- After reading the book, talk some more (e.g., anything about how the story related to the child's experience or life). For example, "Do you know any cats that look like Whiskers?" Talk about your favorite parts of the story. Find out if your child liked the book and wants to hear it again (at a different time).

- Reread stories and books that your child enjoyed. The more your child is familiar with the book, the more he or she will be able to join in and share in the reading. Praise any of your child's attempts and efforts to read books, join in, or "read" to you.

- Encourage your child to retell the story with the beginning, main events, and ending.

- Encourage your child to "read" the book to a favorite doll or stuffed toy.

Additional Help This Book Offers

Other sections of this book address aspects of reading to and with your child. See "Getting Them Off to a Good Start: Strategies for Developing Emergent and Beginning Reading Skills," "What Good Readers Do: Positive Reading Behaviors," "Building Vocabulary and Comprehension Skills," "How to Ask Questions That Guide

Your Child in Developing Good Reading Strategies and Thinking Skills," "What the Experts Say: Interviews with Kindergarten and Preschool Teachers and Directors," "What Research Says about Preventing Reading Difficulties," "The Most Important Gifts You Can Give Your Child," "Creating a Home Environment That Encourages Success," and "Developmentally Appropriate Games, Books, Songs, Manipulatives, and Other Activities/Resources."

Building Vocabulary and Comprehension Skills

Your child's language acquisition and usage is developing at an amazing rate during the early years. There is much that you can do to stimulate this growth and extend your child's vocabulary. There is a high correlation between word knowledge and academic success/ achievement. Knowing the meanings of words obviously affects both listening and reading comprehension in all areas. Those individuals who have facility and confidence with words are more skilled in language usage—with better ability to communicate and express themselves in oral language and written language. This confidence with language affects one's social competence—the ability to interact effectively with others.

Children between the ages of 3 and 5 have a phenomenal capacity for learning language(s). They are like little language sponges. Children learn language(s) from listening to and speaking with the models around them and through the world of words they are exposed to in books and in their daily experiences.

The following strategies will help children increase their knowledge and usage of words (which, in turn, will develop their listening and reading comprehension skills):

• Speak to your child. You are the most important language model in your child's life; have conversations, and use descriptive vocabulary.

- Expand on the language your child is using. For example, if your child says, "That puppy is cute," you can expand by adding more description, such as, "That is an adorable little cocker spaniel puppy. Look at its floppy ears and golden fur."

- Play guessing games with your child that require using specific, descriptive vocabulary to categorize or describe an object in order to guess it. For example, "I'm thinking of something in the refrigerator that I slice with a knife to put in salads. It is red, juicy, and has a smooth skin. What is it?"

- Look through picture books, picture dictionaries, and magazines, talking about the pictures of objects, actions, and scenes and using descriptive language to do so. When looking at a book, for example, say, "Oh look at the cows grazing in the pasture. Here comes the cowboy galloping on his horse. Do you know what he's holding and twirling over his head?"

- Talk about words that are unfamiliar when reading together, explaining what things mean to your child and using synonyms when possible to explain unfamiliar vocabulary (e.g., *tired* for *exhausted, happy* for *delighted)*. Reading greatly enhances vocabulary development.

- Explain that some words have different meanings even though they sound and sometimes look exactly the same (e.g., *fare/fair, hair/hare, sent/cent/scent, punch/punch, fall/fall, strike/strike)*. Give examples of how they are used in context.

- Point out objects your child may not be familiar with in the environment; talk about them and name them.

- Play classification games. For example, "lettuce, cucumbers, carrots, broccoli, corn are all . . . vegetables."

- Use descriptive vocabulary in everyday experiences. For example, describe the tastes of foods (*spicy, salty, sweet, sour, bitter)*, describe textures or how things feel (*smooth, rough, bumpy, scratchy, slimy)*, describe sounds (*screeching, thumping, loud, soft, soothing, whistling)*, and so forth.

• Teach prepositions by playing games and pointing out relationship words whenever possible. These are very important vocabulary words and concepts your child will need to know for school readiness and the ability to follow directions. Through all kinds of activities together, help your child to understand words such as *beneath, below, under, near, next to, over, around, in between, above, inside, outside, on top of, beside.*

• Teach the vocabulary that describes feelings and emotions. Development of social skills requires being able to perceive how others are feeling by the looks on their faces and their body language. Also, children need to learn how to express their emotions appropriately through language (not through their fists). Teach your child the words for emotions and feelings (e.g., "I'm feeling angry . . . worried . . . frightened . . . upset . . . sad.").

• Whenever possible, and through the context of conversation and activities, teach the meanings of and use of vocabulary such as body parts (e.g., *neck, elbows, knees, ankles),* shapes (e.g., *circle, triangle, square),* measurement (e.g., *thermometer, calendar, scale, half, whole),* and so forth.

• There are wonderful books that focus on specific vocabulary awareness and usage. For example, the book *Polar Bear, Polar Bear, What Do You Hear* (by Bill Martin, Jr., and Eric Carle, New York: Henry Holt & Co., 1991) introduces children to words such as *hissing, snorting, snaring, whistling* through the context of the delightful text and illustrations.

• If your family's primary language is other than English, speak it in the home and teach it to your child. Those who are bilingual or multilingual have the greatest advantages in our multicultural world. We all know the value and benefits of being able to communicate in a second language. So, nurture and encourage your child's development of both your native/primary language as well as English.

The relationship between reading and vocabulary is an interesting one. The more text you read, the more words you are exposed to, and the more vocabulary you learn. The more vocabulary you know, the stronger and more proficient you become as a reader. On the other hand, you need to know vocabulary in order to read. It is hard to read independently, and discouraging to do so, when many of the words on the page are unfamiliar to you in meaning; when you can't anticipate while reading what word(s) might make sense; and when decoding an unfamiliar word in print that isn't one you have heard used before. Research shows that the number of words in print that a child is exposed to is a significant factor in how well the child will be able to read. Good readers are exposed to many, many more words in print than poor readers. That is why children need to be read to as much as possible from an early age. Once your child has enough skills to start reading simple books on his or her own, it is important to provide the opportunity and encouragement to do so as often as possible (in addition to reading to your child).

Additional Help This Book Offers

For additional strategies to build vocabulary and comprehension skills, see the sections "Playing with Sounds and Language," "Language and Literacy: The Building Blocks of School Success," "Getting Them Off to a Good Start: Strategies for Developing Emergent and Beginning Reading Skills," "The Importance of Read-Alouds and Shared Reading: Strategies for Reading *to* and *with* Your Child," "How to Ask Questions that Guide Your Child in Developing Good Reading Strategies and Thinking Skills," and "Developmentally Appropriate Games, Books, Songs, Manipulatives, and Other Activities/ Resources."

How to Ask Questions That Guide Your Child in Developing Good Reading Habits and Thinking Skills

While reading to and with your child, pause from time to time—not so much that you lose the focus or momentum of the story—to ask questions that engage your child in thinking about the story and making predictions and personal connections. For example,

"What do you think will happen next?"

"Can you guess what might be behind the door?"

"What do you think he's going to do now?"

"Do you think she made a good choice?"

"Has that ever happened to you?"

"How would you feel if you were ____?"

"Where do you think ____ might hide?"

"If that happened to you, how would you feel?"

"Why do you think she's doing that?"

"What would you do if you were ____?"

"Did you ever feel that way?"

"Why do you think he looks so ____?"

"Did you like this story?"

"What's your favorite part?"

"Why do you think ____ said that?"

"What was the funniest part?"

"Do you know what that word ____ means?"

"What's happening in this picture?"

"Who does that remind you of?"

"How can you tell that . . . ?"

Make comments that focus your child's attention to different aspects of the story. For example,

"I wonder where ____ is going."

"Let's find out why . . ."

"I think I know what's going to happen next."

"Oh, look at the . . ."

"I wonder what ____ is going to do now."

"I wonder how the story will end."

When your child is able to read simple books to himself or herself and out loud to you and gets stuck on a word, there are several strategies you can use. One is to supply the word your child doesn't know. That is fine to do. It is also very helpful to assist and guide your child in the process of figuring out unfamiliar words by asking certain questions and prompting through the use of cueing strategies:

1. *Graphophonic cues*—looking at the letters/sounds of the word. For example, check the initial letter/sound of the word and other additional sounds or parts of the word that the child may know. Prompt and ask questions such as "Look at the beginning of the word. What's that sound?" "What does the letter ___ say?"

2. *Semantic cues*—listening to hear if a word makes sense. Ask questions such as "Does that make sense? Can the boy run *fat*? What other word would make sense?"

3. *Syntactic cues*—listening to make sure it sounds right. "Does that sound like we talk? Do we say, 'I going to bed?' Go back and read that sentence again."

Prompt your child to determine if a misread word looks right, sounds right, and makes sense. When stuck on a word, your child can skip over that word and read to the end of the sentence. Often by the end of the sentence your child will figure out the missed word through clues from the context of the other words or illustration on the page. Encourage your child through comments and prompts such as, "You made a really good guess on that word. ___ makes sense. But look at the beginning of the word. Could that word be ___? What else could it be?"

Your child has a natural curiosity about his or her world. Nurture that eagerness to discover and learn whenever the opportunity arises—not just through reading. Take the time to talk to your child about all the things he or she is wondering about. Ask questions like "Why do you think . . . ?" "How should we . . . ?" "What do you think about . . . ?" "What do you guess will happen if . . . ?" Doing so will not only build your child's expressive language, thinking, and reasoning skills, but will also solidify your loving, caring relationship. Your child will know that you are interested in his or her questions and in how he or she thinks and feels.

Beginning Phonics, Word Recognition, and Word Study Skills

During the kindergarten year emergent readers and writers are being taught beginning phonics and word recognition skills. This section discusses the terminology and types of beginning phonics and word recognition skills children need to become independent readers and writers. Before your child is developmentally capable of understanding or applying any phonics or word recognition, he or she needs to have developed phonological awareness and alphabet knowledge. See the sections "What Is Phonemic and Phonological Awareness?" "Playing with Sounds and Language," and "Helping Your Child Learn the Alphabet."

Phonology refers to the way sounds of the language operate—the general ability to attend to the sounds of language as distinct or separate from its meaning. Children need to be able to hear and attend to the different sounds of spoken language before they have the ability to begin reading or writing. As is explained in the sections "What Is Phonemic and Phonological Awareness" and "What Research Says about Preventing Reading Difficulties," the awareness that words are made up of a series of distinct, separate sounds that are blended together sequentially is critical to learning how to read or write. This has nothing to do with being able to recognize printed words—it is a completely auditory process.

The conscious insight that spoken words are made up of a sequence of individual sounds (called *phonemes*) and being able to play around with or manipulate those separate sounds is referred to as *phonemic awareness.* It involves being able to hear and recognize when words rhyme (e.g., the words *Kate* and *eight*). It also involves hearing (not seeing) the word *sun* and being able to identify that the word *sun* is composed of three sounds—/s/ /u/ /n/; or *night,* which also has three distinct sounds—/n/ /i/ /t/. Another phonological skill and part of phonemic awareness is the ability to hear what the whole word is if you were to say it slowly and stretched out. For example, if you were to say, *rrrraaaannn,* your child would be able to identify that word as *ran.* If you were to say, *sssiiit,* your child would recognize that word as *sit.* Sounds that are easiest for children to hear are the ones that can be held and extended continuously without being distorted. The mouth stays in the same position, and that sound can be held indefinitely or at least until one runs out of breath. This includes sounds such as */ffffff/, /rrrrrr/, /mmmmmm/, /ssssss/, /aaaaa/, /llllll/,* and so forth. Other sounds (called "stop sounds") are harder to hear because they are pronounced very quickly. These include sounds like */b/, /k/, /d/, /p/, /t/.* So it is better when first doing this kind of activity with your child to start with words that have continuous sounds that you can hold such as *run (/rrrrrr/uuuuuuu/nnnnnn/)* rather than words like *tip (/t/ /iiiiii/ /p/).**

Research shows that struggling readers and writers in the early grades have commonly not acquired these important phonological awareness skills. Other important skills include hearing the number of words within a sentence, such as saying simple sentences and having your child be able to clap or count out the number of words he or she hears in the sentence. For example, "I am going shopping" (four words). Another skill for phonological awareness development is counting out the syllables in words that are spoken (e.g., hap•py—

---

*In our book *Alphabet Learning Center Activities Kit* (authored by Nancy Fetzer and Sandra Rief, Paramus, NJ: The Center for Applied Research in Education, 2000), we refer to continuous sounds as "holders," and the sounds that can't be held or extended as "fasties." There is a start and stop to the fastie sounds; and the mouth (position of lips and tongue) changes during the production of those sounds. The alphabet cues we introduce to children with the Holder and Fastie Alphabet help children learn each of the letter sounds by calling attention to the feel of the sounds and where they are made in the mouth.

two syllables, el•e•phant—three syllables). The section "Playing with Sounds and Language" contains many fun activities and games that are helpful in the development of phonological awareness.

Of course, reading and writing require alphabet knowledge. However, your child does not have to know *all* of the letters of the alphabet in order to begin reading or writing. There are different components of alphabet knowledge that you should expose your child to (when he or she seems interested and ready). Refer to the section "Helping Your Child Learn the Alphabet." If your child is approaching kindergarten or is in kindergarten, you may wish to see the sections "What Are General Kindergarten Readiness Skills?" and "Kindergarten Performance Standards." These sections may give you a better idea of what is expected of children in terms of reading and writing skills.

Your child will need to develop letter/sound association skills—the ability to see a printed letter of the alphabet and identify it by name and by its sound as well as vice versa—hear a letter name or sound and locate the printed letter. It is much more important to be able to match the letter to the sound than it is to be able to say the letter's name. Your child will need to know the difference between capital or upper-case letters such as *A, B, C . . .* and the lower-case letters *(a, b, c . . .)* and be able to match them (e.g., *G/g, I/i*). Knowing the letter/sound association for the alphabet letters is not easy for children who have difficulty with phonological awareness. Expose your child to this concept through ABC books, picture dictionaries, looking at magazines together, and pointing out objects in the environment. For example, "The letter *c* says /k/ like *cat, cup, cake, crayon, corn, cookie, candy, coat.*" "The letter *m* says /m/ like *mouse, milk, monkey, man.*" A more advanced level involves being able to identify the sounds at the end of the word, such as *"bus* and *kiss* end with the /s/ sound, *cat* and *sit* end with the /t/ sound."

When children start acquiring the knowledge of letter/sound associations, or what is also called print-sound code, and applying that knowledge to "sound out" words in print, they have learned what is referred to as *phonics.* The skill of seeing an unfamiliar word in print and applying what is known about the letters and their sounds to decipher the word is called *decoding.*

Children acquire letter/sound knowledge through learning a progression of skills. Initially children learn to recognize the letter/sound association for the consonant letters (*b, c, d, f, g, h, j, k, l, m, n, p, q, r, s, t, v, w, x, y, z*) and vowels *(a, e, i, o, u)*. Most teachers introduce the letters not in alphabetical order but by frequency. They start by teaching a group of consonants that are common in print and are found in a number of words the children typically use. They also teach only one vowel first (generally the *a* as in *apple)* and then later introduce another, and then another. As mentioned earlier, children can start reading and writing without first knowing all of the letters of the alphabet or their sounds. Once they know a few common consonants (e.g., *b, c, f, l, m, n, p, r, s, t*) and one vowel, a number of two- or three-letter words can be put together for reading and writing (e.g., *bat, am, can, cat, rat, nap, tan, cap, fan, cab, Sam, man, ran, sat*). Of course, when a second vowel (such as *i)* is introduced and a few more consonants (e.g., *d, g, h*), quite a few words are able to be generated and played with in reading and writing (e.g., *bit, sip, fin, big, Dan, sad, gas, hid, hat, has, dig, Tim)*. *Note:* Try not to confuse your beginning readers by introducing words at this time that make a different vowel sound from what they have been taught so far. For example, if your child knows the sound of *a* as in *hat, ran, cap,* practice with words that make that regular sound of the short *a.* Avoid words like *far* or *call,* which are confusing because the letter *a* in those words makes a different vowel sound. If your child is able to start building two- or three-letter words for reading and writing and has the interest in doing so, use manipulative letters (such as magnetic letters on a refrigerator or those made from colored foam, felt, plastic, sponge, etc.) to create these words.

Word study is a term that educators use to refer to the process of learning how the written language system works. Children are taught not only to attend to the individual letters in a word when reading and spelling, but to also notice the common spelling patterns or groups of letters that go together (such as *ight* in words like *night, right, fight,* and so forth). Beginning readers are taught to look for chunks within words (e.g., consonant digraphs such as *ch, th, sh,* beginning blends such as *st, br, sm, fl,* final blends such as *-nd,-mp,-st,* and inflectional endings such as *-ing,-s,-ed*). They are taught to look for smaller words within words (e.g., compound words such as *girl-friend, snowfall*).

During the kindergarten year children are only expected to be able to decode some simple, one-syllable words. Even in first grade, teachers begin instruction with three-letter words that follow the basic consonant-vowel-consonant (C-V-C) pattern found in words like *cat* and *big* before progressing to the more advanced word patterns.

Words that rhyme and have the same simple spelling pattern are good words for beginning readers to start looking at and focusing on in word study. Children are taught to see the patterns in print in word families such as the *at* family (e.g., *sat, mat, pat, rat, hat cat*), the *ig* family *(big, wig, dig)*, the *ad* family *(bad, sad, had, mad, pad, Dad)*. You may hear teachers refer to onset and rimes. Rimes are the part of a word including the vowel and the letters that follow (e.g., *-at,-ill,-op*). Onsets are the letters that come in front of the first vowel of the rime. To help children recognize the patterns of all the different words with the same ending sounds and spellings, it is helpful to play games substituting the onsets (or beginning letters) and keeping the rime the same. For example, start with *cat,* which is made from the onset *c* and the rime *at.* Change the beginning letter or onset to *p* to make *pat,* and change the *p* to *f* and make *fat.* Change the *f* to *s* and make *sat,* and so forth.

Again, you don't want to push your child to learn these skills until he or she is ready. If you rush these skills, your child may become frustrated and discouraged. This could be harmful in early literacy development and to your child's self-esteem, especially those that are fragile. Consult with your child's teacher as to how you can best help your developing reader and writer.

Many of the words your beginning reader will be encountering in print are phonetically regular—meaning that they are spelled exactly the way they sound (e.g., *man, slip, hand*). The printed letters match each of the sounds heard within the words. Once your child knows the sounds for the letters and how to blend them together, these words can be decoded accurately by "sounding them out." It is important to give beginning readers practice reading text that is easy to decode. This builds their confidence in being independent readers.

Other words cannot be "sounded out" and need to be recognized by sight, such as *the, said, you, was, they, of, what, why.* By the end of the kindergarten year, most school districts expect children to know about twenty-five basic sight words. These are taught through frequent exposure and practice—using flashcards of a few words at a time until recognized and said quickly and automatically, games of various kinds, circling, color highlighting or marking in some way the targeted word(s) when seen in print within the environment. In *Alphabet Learning Center Activities Kit,* we refer to those high-frequency sight words that teachers target for a grade level as "expert words" that they need to be able to read "as fast as a snap."

Your child will eventually become an independent reader as he or she gains competence in word identification skills—in applying phonetic strategies to "sound out" words, in recognizing patterns and chunks within words to help figure out an unknown word (e.g., "I know *th* and *ing,* so that must be *thing*"), and in rapidly identifying a number of sight words. Being able to read requires the ability to decode words quickly in the text. These are critical skills taught in the early grades and encompass a significant portion of first-grade reading instruction.

PART 5

Getting Your Child Organized and Ready for Writing, Math, and Homework

There are a number of ways parents can help their preschooler and kindergartner on the road to becoming proficient writers. There are three sections in this part of the book that provide information about how young children learn to write along with numerous strategies for helping your child develop these skills. Children pass through predictable stages as they develop into fluent writers. Your preschooler will be in the prewriting and emergent stage and then progress, generally during the second half of kindergarten or first grade, into the beginning-level stage of writing development. See *What to Expect in the Emergent and Beginning Levels of Writing Development* and *Getting Them Off to a Good Start: Strategies for Developing Emergent and Beginning Writing Skills.*

The physical act of writing is one involving fine motor skills—the ability to control fine muscle movements in order to hold and manipulate a crayon, pencil, or other writing tool. See the section *Strategies for Building Fine Motor and Prewriting/Writing Skills* for lots of fun ways to help your child strengthen and develop these important fine motor skills.

Your child's budding mathematical abilities develop through play, exploration, and basic everyday activities. Again, there are many fun ways and activities through which you can help your child acquire mathematical awareness. See the sections *Beginning Number and Mathematical Concepts* and *Helping Your Child Develop Critical Math Skills and Concepts.*

As your child advances through his or her future school years, organization, time management, study skills, and homework will be necessary for school success. Of course, in these early years your child isn't developmentally ready and can't be expected to be organized or to understand time concepts and/or time management. However, it isn't too early to plant the seeds and begin to develop some good habits that will serve your child well in the future. See the sections *Beginning Time Awareness and Organizational Skills* and *The Value and Purpose of Homework.*

What to Expect in the Emergent and Beginning Levels of Writing Development

Children pass through predictable stages as they develop eventually into fluent writers. Your preschooler will be in the prewriting and emergent stage and then progress generally sometime during the second half of the kindergarten year or first grade into the beginning-level stage of writing development—at which time the child is using written language effectively to communicate with others for a number of purposes.

By viewing you and other adults and older children writing, your child will imitate or mimic you and pretend to write, scribbling random marks on a page. Without yet knowing the alphabet or understanding that letters represent the sounds they say, and those groups of letters separated by spaces represent the words they hear and say, children know that writing is important. As children develop in their awareness of the concept of print and in fine motor control, scribbles and marks may more closely resemble print and be written left to right and top to bottom on a page.

As the child learns some letters and can either copy or remember them, he or she will start writing them. Often the first letters the child writes are those in his or her name. Strings of random letters (without spacing between them) occur developmentally at this emergent stage. This is typical of what you would expect to see early in the kindergarten year along with a picture the child draws.

As the child acquires the knowledge of some letter/sound association, he or she will begin to represent some words by writing the beginning sounds for those words. It becomes common to soon see words represented by their initial sounds (i.e., *l* for *like,* or *p* for *pretty*), some spacing between these "words," along with a few real words the child either knows how to write or can copy. This is what you may expect to see along with a picture to go with the child's "story" by the middle of the kindergarten year.

As children develop more awareness that words are made up of a sequence of sounds represented by letters, and they learn more and more letters and their corresponding sounds, they start stringing those sounds together when they write—utilizing increasingly sophisticated invented spellings that can be deciphered and read by others. Invented spelling (also called developmental spelling or temporary spelling) is what children use in their attempt to write down the sounds of the words they hear. Generally, consonant sounds are the dominant sounds the child hears and uses first. For example, the word *hammer* may be written as *hmr;* the word *horse* might be written as *hs; please* may be spelled as *plez.* Invented spellings can be very close approximations to real spelling (e.g., *favorite* as *favrit*). As children develop in their writing skills, their use of correct writing and spelling of some basic high-frequency words (e.g., *the, I, is, my, see, look, to*) increases.

During kindergarten, children should be developing the understanding that the purpose of writing is to communicate a message that can be read and shared. They write "stories," which can be just one sentence or a few, to accompany the pictures they draw. They are labeling objects. They are writing very simple informational pieces (e.g., "My Family" or "All About . . ."). Children are encouraged to write lists, letters, and notes and apply functional purposes for writing frequently throughout the day. They are also responding in simple writing form to something they read in class (e.g., a favorite part in a story, some trait about a character).

Kindergarten curriculum includes teaching children not only to recognize with automaticity and know the sounds for the letters of the alphabet, but also to write correctly all of the letters of the alphabet (upper- and lower-case). Children are typically taught to use lower-case letters in writing words and to use capital letters at the beginning of a name and beginning of a sentence. However, it is common at this stage of writing development for children to mix upper- and lower-case letters within a word. Children are also taught about final punctuation marks. By the end of kindergarten many may remember to use periods, but it is common that they insert the periods at the end of the line, not at the end of the sentence.

At the beginning of the kindergarten year it is typical that *children write large-size* letters, and generally children are not given lined paper for writing. By the middle to end of kindergarten, children often transition to the use of lined paper and do at least some of their writing on lined paper.

All of the aforementioned writing skills develop at varying times for every child. The section titled "Kindergarten Performance Standards" discusses general expectations for students in the academic areas (including writing) by the end of kindergarten. It may be helpful to you as a parent to know those expectations. Keep in mind, however, the wide range of children's developmental progress and readiness. Some children enter kindergarten already knowing many letters and sounds. Some have a strong aptitude and strength in certain skills, such as phonological awareness, making it easier for them to recognize and play with the sounds of language. Some children seem to be natural-born spellers, able to apply phonetic skills with ease when reading and writing, and recognize and remember how to spell words from sight. They may be quite expressive and sophisticated in their written language. Other children may take much longer to acquire these skills, yet are still within developmental expectations.

Getting Them Off to a Good Start: Strategies for Developing Emergent and Beginning Writing Skills

There are a number of ways parents can help their preschoolers and kindergartners on the road to becoming proficient writers. Probably of most importance is for children to see that their parents place a high value on literacy. The home should be a place where parents and other family members are seen reading and writing daily for a variety of functional purposes, as well as for fun. (See the section "Language and Literacy: The Building Blocks of School Success.") Try the following strategies to help build your child's writing skills:

• Write stories together: Your child draws a picture and dictates his or her story. You write down his or her words and read them back to your child. Variations include using actual photographs taken (e.g., a family birthday party, an outing to the beach) and together writing about the event; or cutting out a picture of interest from a magazine and writing something about the picture.

• If your child is able to write down any words, let him or her do so. If your child can write the beginning sound to represent the word, encourage him or her to do so. Let your child use whatever symbols, invented spelling, or writing attempts possible as well as having you record what the child has to say.

• Provide writing materials and tools and encourage writing or drawing every day. Keep supplies in the home that are accessible and available for drawing and writing (e.g., a variety of crayons, white and colored paper, colored washable markers, paints). Special stamps, envelopes, and stickers are also very motivating supplies for children who want to decorate their invitations, birthday cards, letters, notes, and messages they are "writing" to others.

• Always keep handy some supplies for writing and drawing (e.g., a pad of paper, crayons, pencils) when you go somewhere with your child. You may want to keep a canvas bag or a box with some supplies in the trunk of the car, along with a lap tray. You never know when this may come in handy.

• Set up a desk or table that comfortably fits your child's body size, with feet able to rest on the floor and table height appropriate for hand and arm resting and writing without straining.

• Obtain a child-sized easel for painting, drawing, and/or writing and either a chalkboard (with dustless chalk) or white board (with nontoxic dry-erase markers) mounted at a height that is easy for your child to reach.

• Mount your child's drawings and writings. Hang them up on walls or on the refrigerator. Keep a scrapbook, notebook, or portfolio of your child's drawings and writings. Date the work, and have your child sign his or her name.

• Have your child trace some real words he or she wants to use. Try writing the words lightly in pencil or in yellow marker pen and then have your child trace over the letters.

• When your child draws a picture or scribbles something on paper, ask about it and use questions that encourage the child to elaborate in language and expand on the description or story. For example, "Tell me about your picture. What is the dog's name? Where are the boy and dog going?"

• Have a message board (e.g., dry-erase board) in the home in a visible, easy-to-reach location, for notes and messages to family members. A message board in the child's room is also recommended.

Write simple messages to your youngster with words and/or pictures (e.g., "I love you.").

• When you are observing your child writing, you may encourage spacing between words by having your child place two fingers between words.

• Model and point out directionality when you write by showing your child that you start at the left side and write across the page. When you come to the end of the line, you continue with writing your thought or sentence at the beginning of the next line.

• Model to your child or let your preschooler or kindergartner observe older siblings writing reports by gathering information from a variety of books and other resources (e.g., off the Internet).

• Through reading with your child and talking about characters; the setting of the story; the events; the beginning, middle, and end of the story, and so forth, your child learns "story grammar" or what is included in stories. As your child becomes interested in telling you stories and attempting to write his or her own stories, ask a few leading questions that encourage your child to think about and include those elements. For example, "Where is the rabbit going? Does anybody else live with Snowball? Oh, I wonder what's going to happen next."

• Encourage your child's attempts to imitate adults and older children writing for various purposes (e.g., writing directions or instructions, maps, notes, cards, lists, secret messages, recipes).

Additional Help This Book Offers

• For many activities in helping your child learn the letters of the alphabet, see the section "Helping Your Child Learn the Alphabet."

• For activities to help develop your child's fine motor skills (necessary for writing) and fun, multisensory strategies for learning and reinforcing proper letter formation and spelling of simple words, see the section "Strategies for Building Fine Motor and Prewriting/Writing Skills."

• Writing is dependent on the development of a number of visual processing skills (e.g., visual perception, visual sequencing, visual memory). See recommended visual processing strategies and activities in the section "Children with Learning Disabilities, Attention Deficit Disorders, and Other Special Needs."

• Spelling is dependent on a number of auditory processing skills (e.g., phonological awareness, auditory sequencing and memory). See the many strategies and activities that help to develop these skills in the section "Playing with Sounds and Language" and the auditory processing strategies in the section "Children with Learning Disabilities, Attention Deficit Disorders, and Other Special Needs." Also, read the section "What Is Phonemic and Phonological Awareness?"

Strategies for Building Fine Motor and Prewriting/Writing Skills

The physical act of writing involves fine motor skills—the ability to control fine muscle movements in order to hold and manipulate a pencil or other writing tool. Fine motor skills require muscle tone and strength in the fingers, hands, and arms, and is the result of maturation that cannot be hurried. When the child is ready, the physical act of writing occurs. To remember how to form letters and numerals correctly, your child must be able to differentiate between similar-looking letters (e.g., *m/h, n/h, b/d, u/v*); recall the shape of letters and numerals if there isn't a model available to copy; and recall the sequence and directionality of the strokes that comprise the letters and numerals we write. In addition, writing involves the recording of words that are made up of a sequence of sounds. To write most words (those that are spelled phonetically), your child must simultaneously attend to that sequence of sounds while writing down the corresponding symbols. Writing also involves language expression—being able to express thoughts and ideas in language that can be recorded on paper and that will make sense when read by self or others.

If your child is developmentally immature or delayed in fine motor skills, such as manipulation of small objects, eye-hand coordination, and use of fingers/hands to button, zip, hold a scissors and cut, string beads, etc., you may wish to consult with an occupational therapist—a specialist in this area of development.

The following are fun, hands-on activities that will help build these important skills:

- Stacking blocks
- Stringing beads
- Using lacing or sewing cards
- Using pegboards to make patterns and designs
- Tracing over dotted lines and predrawn lines of various kinds (horizontal, zigzag, curved, circular), as well as tracing basic shapes, letters, numerals
- Cutting with scissors along lines that get progressively more difficult (starting at easiest level for success such as short, straight, thick lines)
- Rolling out shapes and forming objects with clay or Play-Doh™
- Flipping over pennies or other coins as quickly as possible
- Picking up a variety of small objects with fingers (e.g., dried rice, beans, nuts, candy, beads, buttons, cereal)
- Picking up a variety of small objects with tweezers, kitchen tongs, clamps
- Buttoning, zipping, tying shoelaces
- Using tools such as wrench with nuts and bolts, screwdriver
- Using any small office supplies (e.g., mini stapler, hole puncher, paper clamps, and paper clips of various sizes)
- Doing finger exercises (e.g., touching thumb to each of the other fingers on the hand as quickly as possible, wiggling, squeezing, pinching movements of fingers/hands)
- Opening/closing lids to containers (e.g., plastic containers with pop-off lids, jars with twisting lids)
- Playing games such as Lite Brite™, Pick-up-Sticks™, Etch-a-Sketch™, Perfection™
- Playing and constructing with Legos™ of various sizes
- Using a rolling pin to flatten and roll out cookie dough and/or crush cookies or graham crackers into crumbs
- Popping plastic bubble wrap

Tactile strategies—those involving touch and input through the sense of feel—are important for your child's learning. They are especially helpful in learning and practicing the formation of letters and numerals. Utilizing their sense of touch helps children recall the visual image of the letter or numeral, as well as the motor movements required in actually writing the letter or numeral. Simultaneously saying the letter's name and/or sound while tracing is even a stronger reinforcer when learning the letters of the alphabet.

With young children it is best to practice beginning writing with large arm movements. There are many techniques for learning beginning writing skills that are developmentally more appropriate for young children than using paper and pencil:

• Write letters in the air with large muscle movements while giving a verbal prompt. While holding your child's wrist, write in large strokes in the air while talking through the strokes. For example, with the letter B, say, "Start at the top. Straight line down. Back to the top. Sideways smile. Sideways smile." (See the book *Alphabet Learning Centers Activities Kit,* by Nancy Fetzer and Sandra Rief, Paramus, NJ: The Center for Applied Research in Education, 2000). Do the same while writing with two fingers in large strokes on carpet.

• Help your child discriminate between and practice forming different kinds of strokes and movements needed for letter formation (e.g., straight lines down, curves, diagonals, zigzags, push aways, around the bends, trace back ups).

• Write large letters with thick marker pens on pieces of cardboard. Squeeze glue or liquid starch over the outline of the letters. Next, sprinkle any textured material (e.g., glitter, salt, colored sand) on top of the glue or starch, and let it dry. Then have your child trace the strokes in the proper sequence as he or she would write the letter or numeral. The act of tracing with the fingers on a texture helps make a sensory imprint on the brain that increases memory and recall of that letter/numeral formation.

• Trace letters (preferably with two fingers) that are cut out in different textured materials or that are covered with various textures (e.g., colored sand, puff paint, sandpaper).

- Make letter/numeral outlines and cover them (together with your child) with yarn, beans, dry macaroni, sequins, and so forth.

- Write letters in a sandbox with your child's fingers or with a stick.

- Play games in which you write letters or numerals on your child's back with your finger, and your child guesses what letter or number you wrote.

- Write large letters on a carpet square with colored chalk. Have your child use his or her hand as an eraser to rub off the chalk after each letter or number is written.

- Use fingerpaint to practice writing letters or numerals. Also, use frosting or pudding on a paper plate or waxed paper to practice writing with a finger.

- Write large letters or numbers on a dry-erase board with colored dry-erase pens. Then erase by tracing over the strokes in correct sequence of the letter/numeral formation with your child's finger.

- Use shaving cream on a tabletop to write letters or numerals with your child's finger.

- Use a damp sponge or paintbrush dipped in water to write or trace over letters or numbers on a chalkboard.

- Use manipulative letters or numbers for different activities (e.g., alphabet cereal, letter tiles, magnetic letters or numbers).

- Make or purchase stencils of letters, numerals, and basic shapes and have your child trace within the boundaries. Any kind of elevated borders or boundaries can be used (e.g., Wikki-Sticks™, fabric or puff paint, liquid glue).

- Make a green dot to indicate the start point when forming letters and numerals. Use arrows and different colors representing the various strokes and their directionality in the letter/number formations.

For more strategies and activities to build the skills required for writing, see the strategies given under "Visual Processing" in the section "Children with Learning Disabilities, Attention Deficit Disorders, and Other Special Needs."

Beginning Number
and Mathematical Concepts

Children are beginning to develop their awareness of number and math concepts in the preschool years. This happens as they mature and acquire skills that enable them to make discoveries about their world. The following are some of these basic understandings that are the foundation of all mathematics.

Patterns

There are patterns all around us. Patterns help us make sense of our world and enable us to make predictions. Being able to discern and identify patterns is important to the world of mathematics because our number system is built upon patterns. With patterning experiences at all levels from early childhood to older grades, it is important for children not only to recognize a pattern, but to extend the pattern and create their own. Examples of everyday experiences that involve patterns are: body movements/games (e.g., "hop, hop, clap . . . hop, hop, clap . . ." and "stand up, sit down, clap, clap, clap . . . stand up, sit down, clap, clap, clap"), making a train of objects or stringing beads using two or three colors (red, blue, red, blue, red, blue), and building a design (stick, circle, circle, stick, circle, circle).

Sorting, Measurement, and Geometry

In early childhood, children develop the ability to recognize and discriminate among shapes, objects, colors, and so forth. This is a critical skill in life. It is important to allow children every opportunity to play with and manipulate a wide variety of objects. Through touching, feeling, and exploring, children make important discoveries and learn essential concepts. They learn about shapes and notice the different shapes within their environment (e.g., square tiles, circular clocks, rectangular books). An awareness of shapes is necessary for design, construction, all art forms, and reading/writing. It also helps children learn about geometric concepts—that something can be cut in half and fit back together again into a whole. Through hands-on experiences children learn how to sort things by shapes, colors, sizes, and functions/purposes. Sorting is an important skill as it teaches children to observe similarities and differences and to categorize by attributes (e.g., find all the seashells that are smooth, that are pink, that are spotted).

Measurement

This is another critical skill. We need to know about size, distance, volume, and weight to make sense of our world. These concepts, as well as those of time and temperature, begin to develop in early childhood through exploration and physical or hands-on activities. Children need many experiences in measuring and comparing—for example, filling containers with water or sand to see which ones hold more (volume); building towers and measuring which one is longer or the tallest (comparing). These experiences help develop the vocabulary and concepts of colder/hotter, more/less, heavier/lighter, taller/shorter, and so on.

Problem Solving

Understanding of numbers at the abstract, conceptual level is built upon the concrete awareness of number and math concepts. Children progress through stages in learning math—concrete, semi-concrete, and abstract. The typical kindergartner is in the concrete stage and needs objects to manipulate to develop his or her math skills. The concepts of addition and subtraction, and number combinations begin to develop in kindergarten and are a very important and substantial part of any first-grade mathematics curriculum.

Number Sense

This involves being able to count sequentially by rote and to recognize numerals (e.g., when shown the numeral 8, can say the word *eight*). It means counting objects with correct one-to-one correspondence. Some children haven't yet grasped the one-to-one concept of counting and don't understand that one object = one word. If given four blocks, they might count 1, 2, 3, 4, 5, 6 (saying that there are six, not four blocks). Emerging number sense involves a beginning awareness and understanding of quantity (how many), comparison (more/less, bigger/smaller), and conservation of number (the number of objects stays the same even if you mix them up, move them around, or hide them).

Helping Your Child
Develop Critical Math
Skills and Concepts

Your child will grow in his or her budding mathematical abilities through play, exploration, and basic everyday activities. You can best help in this process by nurturing your child's natural curiosity about the world.

One way is to provide the opportunities that let your child build, construct, and play with lots of different objects and materials. Boxes and a variety of containers found around the house are very useful for stacking to build towers, and so forth. These kinds of activities involve mathematical concepts and skills such as counting (the number of blocks or other objects in the tower), comparing heights or lengths (of two different towers), and attention to sizes (stacking from the largest up to the smallest object at the top of the tower). Most important, let your child observe you using numbers and applying math in your daily life (e.g., figuring out how much something will cost, balancing your checkbook, using instruments and tools of measurement in the kitchen and garage, etc.).

Your child will learn many mathematical concepts when you let him or her help you with everyday activities around the house or yard/garden. This is a wonderful opportunity to interact and have fun together while your child discovers the mathematical world in which we live. For example:

• When doing laundry, your child can help sort clothing (by type of clothing, colors, to whom they belong). By talking during this time, your son or daughter can gain in mathematical awareness and vocabulary. Say things like, "Whose pile of clothes is smallest? Who has more socks in the laundry, Kevin or Mommy?" Have your child help you fold some of the towels. Use mathematical vocabulary by saying, "Let's fold this towel in half. Let's make our corners match. Now let's fold it in half again."

• Cooking or baking together provides a wealth of opportunities to stimulate your child's mathematical awareness and development of concepts. For example, when baking chocolate chip cookies, your child can do a lot of counting (e.g., number of chips, number of cookies on the tray). Your child can measure (fill the cup to the top with flour). You can encourage patterning (e.g., fill the cookie sheet in rows with spoonfuls of batter that are big/big/little/big/big/little, or decorate cookies with some pattern). Build the skills of estimation (e.g., "How many chips do you think are in this cookie?") and comparison ("Which plate has the most cookies?" "Show me the biggest and smallest cookie on the plate.") You can even introduce some sophisticated time concepts for young children. ("The cookies are almost done. They will be ready in five more minutes. That's when the timer will beep. Let's see how many songs we can sing in five minutes.")

• When setting the table, ask your child to help you by bringing four napkins, four spoons, four forks (or whatever number is needed for your family).

Here are additional ways to develop critical math skills and concepts:

• Make a game out of looking for objects that have a certain number of items in a set (e.g., two wheels on a bike, two shoes on your two feet; two wings on a bird).

• Help your child with one-to-one correspondence when counting by simultaneously pairing an action while saying each of the numbers. Bounce a ball, clap hands, beat a drum, pound a desk, or do some physical movement as each number is verbalized while counting. It helps to do so in a steady, even rhythm (1...2...3...4). Have your child count while he or she observes you perform some motion (e.g., tap your head, snap your fingers, flip cards over).

- Have puzzles in the home that are simple (not many pieces). An assortment of types and sizes of blocks is also important for child's play and learning.

- Keep handy assorted plastic containers for bathtub play or sand play, which will help your child with the beginning concept of volume.

- Have your child develop the ability to see small sets of objects, identifying quickly "how many" (without one-to-one counting). For example, have three keys (or two pencils or one cracker or four pennies) on the table covered up with a piece of paper or your hand. Uncover briefly—just a quick flash before covering up again—and ask, "How many?" Make a game out of this. Use from one to four sets of objects—no higher. You may even limit the activity to sets of one or two items. If your child has mastered the ability to distinguish between sets of one or two without counting (can look and say quickly if the set has one or two items without having to touch or point to each item and count), then you can try for sets of three.

- Play games that require rolling one die and identifying the number.

- Play simple board games (e.g., Candyland™) that are developmentally appropriate for your child. When your child wants to start counting the space (box) his or her marker is standing on as "one," you can do the following suggested by Jan Semple, author of the *Semple Math Program* (800-343-1211): Boxes on a game board where players place their markers are referred to as "guys." Say, "Don't count the guy you are standing on. He already had a turn. Start with the next guy." This technique is concrete and helps children understand where to begin counting as they move their markers.

- Play games in which your child guesses (predicts) and then compares sizes, shapes, and lengths. For example, have your child guess how long you can stand on one foot before losing balance.

Then start counting as you do so. Have your child guess how many giant steps (distance) it will take him or her to walk from one side of the room to another. Then he or she takes the giant steps while counting. Don't be surprised if your child says a number such as 100 or 1,000 giant steps (when it is only 10). All games of estimation and measurement should be fun and playful. They are exposing children to *skills that are sophisticated and take many years to develop.*

• Play matching games with your child (e.g., finding another object of the same shape, or matching two pictures that have the same number of objects, such as three kittens, three dolls).

• Play games in which you show a number of fingers and ask, "How many?"

• Play comparison games. For example, show five fingers and ask your child to build a tower with linking blocks using that many blocks (five). Then show three fingers. After your child identifies that there are three fingers, ask him or her to build another tower with that many blocks. Now have your child compare the size of the two towers and ask, "Which is more? Which one has fewer?"

• Find cookie cutters in different shapes (stars, circles) and have your child cut out shapes in clay or Play-Doh™. Then ask your child to point to the star; point to the circle.

• Using a limited number of cards with shapes on them (two triangles, two squares, two circles, two diamonds), turn the cards face down on a table top. Keep turning over two at a time and looking for the matches until your child can remember where all the matches are.

• If your child likes to collect things (e.g., rocks, seashells, leaves, stickers), use these items for sorting by characteristics.

• If you are teaching your child to write numerals, ask your child's preschool or kindergarten teacher for any verbal prompts they use. Use the same and reinforce at home. For example, "3–around the tree, around the tree."

Most important, have fun with your child and don't worry or be anxious if your child has difficulty grasping these mathematical concepts. Children are in the concrete stage of development and learn when their senses are involved. They learn how to count by handling items (manipulatives). They learn through play. They are not in an abstract stage of development yet. The abstract language and concepts of mathematics are just beginning to form near the end of the kindergarten years.

Beginning Time Awareness and Organization Skills

One of the most important skills for success throughout the school grades and into adulthood is the ability to organize oneself. This includes organization of materials, work space, and assignments, as well as time management, such as arriving to school on time, meeting deadlines, pacing oneself on assignments, and turning work in on time. It isn't too early to plant the seeds for these important skills in your child. Good habits are developed with practice. The following suggestions will prime your child for success in school:

- Arrange your child's room (bedroom and/or playroom) so that he or she knows where things belong when not in use. By labeling (with pictures) shelves, boxes, baskets, or other storage containers, your child will learn where to locate those items (e.g., toys, blocks, supplies). This makes cleanup faster and easier as well since your child will be able to return things to their correct place.

- Store books in tubs or baskets so your child can reach them easily.

- Have a special work area for your child that is equipped with a child-sized table or desk that fits your child's height. Keep handy and accessible supplies that are developmentally appropriate for your child and that encourage writing, drawing, and creativity.

- Young children like to feel like a "big kid." If they have older siblings, preschoolers often want to "do homework" like their brother and sister do. This is a wonderful habit to instill at a young age. If your preschooler draws a picture and/or scribbles something on a page, that "story" is his or her "homework." Let your child share this "homework" with you. Kindergartners may get assigned some homework (about fifteen minutes per night). Having a "homework time" in the daily routine, even if it is only a few minutes, is helpful in developing habits for school success.

- Time awareness develops as children's cognitive and language skills mature. It takes time for a child to understand vocabulary and concepts such as *later, yesterday, tomorrow, tonight, after lunch.* It takes a great deal longer and much more experience and maturity for a child to understand the concept of *year, month, week, hour, minute, second.*

- We know that young children have no awareness or comprehension of elapsed time (e.g., "in two hours" or "an hour ago") and they have great difficulty waiting for time to pass and understanding how long things take (especially when they are looking forward to something special). For example, if your child's birthday is on Sunday, or in four days . . . most likely your child will ask countless times each day, "Is it Sunday yet?" "How much more till my birthday?" You may wish to have a calendar with the special day colored or indicated with a picture in it, crossing out each day that passes.

- Realize that it takes most children until the upper elementary grades to understand many time concepts, such as telling time to the minute, elapsed time (e.g., "What time will it be in 3 1/2 hours from now?")

- Talk about time in ways that make it concrete and more understandable for your child. For example, "We are going to leave at 4 o'clock. That's when Susie comes back from school." "We're going to eat at 6:30 when it's dark outside and Daddy is home."

By the end of kindergarten most children should be able to demonstrate understanding of morning, afternoon, and night; tell time using calendars (e.g., days of the week, months of the year, seasons); and be able to tell time to the nearest hour. Use those time references when talking to your child about daily events and activities. For example, "Christmas is in December. That's the last month of the year when it is winter and cold outside." Children should be given the opportunity to see analog clocks (ones with minute and hour hands) as well as digital clocks. Consider purchasing one to help your child practice telling time to the hour (e.g., 3:00, 7:00, 9:00).

The Value and Purpose
of Homework

It is helpful if we instill even in very young children the value of taking time each day (afternoon/early evening) to focus on homework. There are many benefits children gain from doing homework: They show higher achievement in academic areas; they learn responsibility, self-discipline, and work ethic; they learn how to find information and apply new skills; and they develop the study habits that are vital for achievement and success.

There are a number of purposes for homework. One is to increase the home/school partnership, which is vital to school success. Research shows that when parents are involved in and show interest in what children are learning in school, children are more successful students. Homework provides an opportunity for parents to see what their children are learning and to demonstrate their support of classroom instruction and learning goals. Homework is a feedback mechanism letting parents and teachers know whether students are grasping the concepts and subject matter being taught. Homework also extends a child's learning by requiring further investigation and creative projects related to what is being taught in class.

Another major purpose of homework is to provide extra practice, review, and reinforcement of skills the child is learning in school. As you can see in the section "Kindergarten Performance Standards," teachers must convey quite a bit of content, skills, and concepts. Often there is not enough time to provide all the practice every child needs to achieve educational goals and standards during the school day. In addition, with a class of twenty children or so it is difficult to observe each child closely every day as he or she is learning letters, numbers, and other skills/concepts. As a parent, you are in a good position to notice if your child is having some difficulty learning or needs more support. We learn new skills through practice. The more your child practices and receives support and encouragement while learning new skills, the better the chances for success. Be aware, though, that the best and most appropriate practice with young children needs to be brief. It is best to practice something frequently but in short intervals.

Once your child is in kindergarten, it is generally expected that he or she will do some homework every day (about fifteen minutes). Be supportive by communicating your expectation that a quiet time is set for study/homework time. If your child doesn't have any assigned work, some quiet activities that enhance learning, such as drawing, writing, and reading, should be encouraged during this time for study.

With all preschoolers and kindergartners, being read to aloud every day by parents, siblings, day-care providers, grandparents, and others is the most valuable and necessary homework for developing literacy.

PART 6

What to Do if You Suspect Your Child Has a Developmental Delay or Disability

You may notice and have concerns that your child appears delayed in some developmental skill areas, or perhaps your child has been diagnosed with a particular disability. It is often the case that children, such as those with learning disabilities, have hidden weaknesses or disabilities that go undetected until they start moving up in the grades with ever-increasing academic and behavioral demands/expectations. It is important to know that there are highly successful adults in every profession and walk of life who have various disabilities and disorders. Many are highly intelligent, creative, and resourceful, and have overcome or compensated for the challenges associated with their disabilities.

We know that with early identification of problem areas and appropriate intervention targeted to address those specific areas of weakness, children with disabilities can be helped considerably. Many potential difficulties can be prevented or at least reduced significantly. Skills can be developed and improved dramatically with proper intervention and effective strategies. There is much that can be done to achieve a positive prognosis and outcome for children with disabilities. Many of the strategies, techniques, and kinds of supports children need are simple and fun, not to mention very doable for parents in collaboration and partnership with the professionals.

Children with disabilities are entitled under federal law to special education programs, related services, and supports to meet their needs. Parents have rights and a range of free and appropriate program/service options for their child guaranteed under federal law. It is important that if you are concerned and suspect your child has a disability, that you know your rights and be able to access the help your child may need.

This part of the book provides such information and guidance. See the sections *When You Are Concerned About Your Child's Development* and *Working with Your Child's School: A Team Approach.*

There is also a section describing a variety of disabilities in children including the following: attention deficit hyperactivity disorder (ADHD), communication disorders, visual and other physical disabilities, mental retardation and multiple disabilities, pervasive developmental disorders (e.g., autism), emotional and/or behavioral disabilities (e.g., oppositional defiant disorder), health impairments and other disorders (e.g., Tourette's syndrome), and specific learning disabilities. Under the category of *Specific Learning Disabilities* you will find information and activities to help with visual and auditory processing deficits.

Children with Learning Disabilities, Attention Deficit Disorders, and Other Special Needs

You may have specific concerns about your child due to your observations of or a diagnosis of some developmental weaknesses. Perhaps you are concerned because other family members, immediate or extended family, have learning disabilities, ADHD, or other disorders/disabilities. The intent of this section is to share general information about common disabilities as well as coping strategies and activities. You should discuss any specific concerns about your child with your child's doctor, teacher, and other appropriate specialists.* (See the section "If You Are Concerned About Your Child's Development.")

Depending on the child and the severity of symptoms, some disabilities or disorders are diagnosed in very early childhood.

However, often it isn't until a youngster is in elementary school—usually first or second grade—that the child's difficulties become apparent. The expectations and demands of the school environment at that time—academic, behavioral, social/emotional—are such that the child has difficulty performing as other children of that grade level do. Parents and teachers become more aware that perhaps something is "wrong," as the child is clearly struggling to cope

---

*Children with health impairments and disorders that adversely affect the child's ability to learn and function well in school may be eligible for a range of accommodations, supports, and/or services. Consult with your school nurse and other specialists at school, as well as your child's health-care providers.

and compensate for his or her weaknesses. This is often the time when parents or teachers will initiate the process of seeking help, to diagnose the problem and to provide additional support and intervention for the child.

Attention Deficit Hyperactivity Disorder

Attention deficit hyperactivity disorder (ADHD, also known as ADD or attention deficit disorder) is believed to be a neurobiological disorder characterized by developmentally abnormal degrees of inattention, impulsivity, and hyperactivity. ADHD often interferes with a child's ability to function with success academically, behaviorally, and/or socially, and it affects approximately 3 to 5 percent of the population. There are different subtypes of the disorder, which are all classified under the umbrella term *attention deficit hyperactivity disorder.* ADHD is often described by the medical/scientific community as a neurological inefficiency in the area of the brain that controls impulses, aids in screening sensory input, and focuses attention. Children with ADHD typically have great difficulty inhibiting their behaviors and impulses. They are often extremely active and distractible, with much shorter attention spans for most tasks than other children their age; and due to their impulsivity, they are prone to accidents and injury. *Note:* If your child can focus for a long time on activities such as playing with Legos™ or electronic games like Nintendo™, it doesn't mean that he or she couldn't have ADHD. Those tasks are highly motivating, novel, and constantly changing. Children with ADHD can often be attentive and focus on those kinds of activities yet are unable to attend to most other tasks for more than a few minutes at the most.

There are countless strategies (and wonderful resources) that parents and teachers can employ that make a big difference in how well a child with ADHD is able to function and perform. Books and videos on this topic that may be of interest to parents include:

Barkley, Russell. *ADHD: What Can We Do?* (videotape). New York: Guilford Press Video, 1993.

Flick, Grad L. *Power Parenting for Children with ADD/ADHD*. Paramus, NJ: The Center for Applied Research in Education, 1996.

Reimers, Cathy, and Bruce A. Brunger. *ADHD in the Young Child: A Guide for Parents and Teachers of Young Children with ADHD*. Plantation, FL: Specialty Press, 1999.

Rief, Sandra F. *How to Reach and Teach ADD/ADHD Children*. Paramus, NJ: The Center for Applied Research in Education, 1993.

——— *The ADD/ADHD Checklist*. Paramus, NJ: Prentice Hall, 1997.

——— *How to Help Your Child Succeed in School* (videotape). San Diego, CA: Educational Resource Specialists, 1997.

Children with ADHD may or may not be eligible for special education. It depends on the impact of the ADHD—how much it adversely affects the child's ability to learn and perform in school.

Communication Disorders

Communication disorders include those that affect and interfere with one or more of the processes involved in communication: hearing, speech (e.g., articulation, fluency, abnormal voice), and language (receptive, which is the ability to understand language, and/or expressive, which is the ability to express oneself verbally). If a hearing impairment and/or specific speech or language disorder adversely affects a child's educational performance, the child would qualify for special education services (e.g., speech/language therapy, audiological services). Early diagnosis and intervention for problems with hearing and/or speech/language disorders are very important during the language acquisition years of early childhood. If you are concerned about your child's hearing, speech, or language, seek professional help for your child immediately. See "Auditory Processing Deficits," "Ways to Communicate So Your Child Will Better Listen and Pay Attention," "What Is Phonemic and Phonological Awareness?" and "Playing with Sounds and Language." These sections contain information and strategies that will help you help your child.

Visual and Other Physical Disabilities

Children may have significant visual, physical, or orthopedic disabilities that impair their learning and entitle them to special education services, such as vision therapy, adapted physical education, orientation and mobility services, Braille, printed materials that are modified to be more easily seen and read (e.g., enlarged type), reader services, and/or access and use of various assistive technology as determined by the team and designated in the child's Individualized Education Plan (IEP). Of course, children with orthopedic disabilities are entitled under U.S. law to accommodations such as wheelchair access within the school environment and on the bus. Other special education programs and services are also available as deemed necessary, such as physical and occupational therapy and health/nursing services.

Mental Retardation and Multiple Disabilities

The Individuals with Disabilities Education Act defines mental retardation as "significantly subaverage general intellectual functioning existing concurrently with deficits in adaptive behavior and manifested during the developmental period that adversely affects a child's educational performance" (IDEA, 1997). Children with mild, moderate, severe, or profound levels of mental retardation and those with multiple disabilities—one of which is mental retardation—are eligible for special education programs and services. As is the case with all types and categories of disabilities, and as mandated by federal law, school districts must provide special education programs and placements in the "least restrictive environment" in a manner appropriate to the needs of all students affected by the educational placement.

Pervasive Developmental Disorders

Pervasive developmental disorders (PDD) include autism and autism spectrum disorders such as Asperger's syndrome. As with other developmental and neurobiological disorders, children with autism and related disorders range from high to low functioning, and the prognosis is best with early intervention. Autism is a severe developmental disorder that typically appears during the first three years of life and is characterized by impairment in the broad areas of social interaction, communication, and stereotyped patterns of behavior.

Examples of possible symptoms in the social interaction category include failure to develop peer relationships appropriate to the child's developmental level; trouble relating to or showing responsiveness and interest in other people, including parents and other family members; lack of social or emotional reciprocity; and marked impairment in the use of nonverbal behaviors (e.g., eye contact, body posture, facial expression). In early childhood, autistic children seem happiest when left alone and occupying themselves without reaching out to others or being accessible to others.

Examples of possible symptoms in the area of communication include delay in or lack of spoken language, peculiar speech patterns, flat tone when speaking, marked impairment in the ability to initiate and engage in conversation, significant expressive language difficulty, stereotyped and repetitive use of language, and lack of or little spontaneous make-believe or imaginative play.

Examples of stereotyped patterns of behavior—or what can be considered compulsions and obsessions—include preoccupation with one or more interests that is abnormal either in intensity or focus, inflexible adherence to specific routines or rituals, repetitive motor mannerisms (e.g., hand or finger flapping or twisting), and persistent preoccupation with parts of objects.

It is difficult to assess the cognitive level of children with autism, and in many areas they appear to have low cognitive development. However, it is not uncommon among autistic individuals to have savant skills—exceptional, extraordinary areas of strength and ability that are mind boggling to the average person (e.g., mathematical ability, musical prowess, photographic recall of large amounts of information).

Children with Asperger's syndrome or Asperger's disorder have autistic-like behaviors and marked deficiencies in social and communication skills. They often have obsessive routines, are rigid and avoid changes, and may be preoccupied with a particular subject of interest. As with autism, they have difficulty with nonverbal communication (e.g., avoiding eye contact) and exhibit behaviors that seem odd and eccentric. Many view Asperger's as high-functioning autism or a milder form of autism; others see it as separate from autism. With Asperger's syndrome, language development seems fairly normal; in fact, vocabulary may be quite strong. However, there are generally more subtle language weaknesses (e.g., being very literal and missing humor, peculiar voice and inflection conversational skills). Children with Asperger's syndrome tend to be clumsy. Cognitive development is average, and the child may possess an exceptional skill or talent.

Until fairly recently, there was very little awareness, even among educators, of pervasive developmental disorders (PPD) and autism spectrum disorders. Fortunately, this is beginning to change. We are gaining in our understanding of these disorders and how to best meet the needs of these children. As with any child with a disability that interferes with school achievement, children with PPD or autism spectrum disorders are entitled to special education services, including a range of programs, placements, and service options. An increasing number of children with PPD are being taught in general education classes with various supports and special education services.

Emotional and/or Behavioral Disabilities

There are a number of emotional and behavioral disorders in children that interfere with their ability to learn, perform, and function in school. Emotional disabilities may include depression, anxiety disorders, and other mental problems. IDEA 1997 defines *emotional disturbance* as "a condition exhibiting one or more of the following characteristics over a long period of time and to a marked degree that adversely affects a child's educational performance:

a. An inability to learn that cannot be explained by intellectual, sensory, or health factors

b. An inability to build or maintain satisfactory interpersonal relationships with peers and teachers

c. Inappropriate types of behavior or feelings under normal circumstances

d. A general pervasive mood of unhappiness or depression

e. A tendency to develop physical symptoms or fears associated with personal or school problems."

Children who are diagnosed as having an emotional disability under the IDEA eligibility criteria are entitled to special education programs and services, including a range of placement, program, and service options to best meet the needs of the student. If your child has an emotional disorder, you will also want your child under the care of mental health specialists who are experienced and knowledgeable in the treatment of childhood emotional disorders (e.g., child psychiatrist, child psychologist).

Some behavioral disorders include oppositional defiant disorder (ODD) and conduct disorder, both of which may significantly affect the child's ability to perform and function successfully in school. Oppositional defiant disorder is characterized by hostile, negative, and defiant behaviors with both peers and adults. The behaviors are more frequent, intense, and severe than those of other children that age, and the oppositional/defiant behaviors have been constant and persistent for at least six months. Behaviors indicative of ODD include the following: loses temper very easily; is irritable, argumentative, resistant, and noncompliant; deliberately ignores, and disobeys parents and other adults; is disrespectful; and blames others.

Conduct disorder is a more severe form of oppositional behavior that generally appears during adolescence. It is characterized by a persistent pattern of behavior that intrudes on and violates the basic rights of others without concern or fear of implications. Other behaviors include vandalism, stealing, cruelty to animals, fire setting, and aggression. *Note:* Oppositional defiant disorder and conduct disorder often co-occur with other disorders, such as attention deficit hyperactivity disorder.

When children show signs of behavioral problems that are beyond what would be considered normal for children that age, parents must seek professional assistance and intervention. These children will need parents to be equipped with appropriate and effective behavioral strategies that are proactive and not reactive. For example, you can learn how to prevent problems or reduce behavioral issues by knowing how to state a request or give directions in a way that a child is more likely to comply. Find mental health practitioners (i.e., child psychiatrist, child psychologist) who are experienced, knowledgeable, and skilled in the area of ADHD, ODD, and other disorders that manifest themselves in very challenging behaviors of childhood.

Children with behavioral disorders are not necessarily eligible for special education programs or services, even when those behavioral problems significantly impair learning and functioning in school. Behavioral disorders are not recognized under federal law as entitling a child to special education under IDEA. Some states do provide special education when behavior is the child's primary handicapping condition.

Health Impairments and Other Disorders (including Tourette's Syndrome)

There are a number of health impairments that can cause a child to have difficulties in school (e.g., becoming easily fatigued, having a hard time focusing and maintaining attention, lacking strength and stamina). There are also a variety of other disorders that are generally comorbid with (co-occurring or coexisting with) and often related to other more common disorders such as ADHD. Tourette's syndrome (TS) is one such disorder whose symptoms may emerge during childhood. Many children with TS also have ADHD. TS is classified as a tic disorder. The characteristics or behaviors associated with it are motor and vocal tics, which may be exhibited in different forms and to a range of degrees (mild, moderate, severe). Examples of vocal tics include behaviors such as repetitive grunting or snorting sounds, clearing of throat, barking noises, and a variety of other noises that appear to be made involuntarily. Motor tics are involuntary movements that are repetitive and have no apparent purpose. These might include behaviors such as opening/ closing the mouth, facial grimaces, knee jerking, twitching kind of head movements, and rapid and repeated eye blinking. Tics that are more complex, inappropriate, and disruptive are rare but may also develop (e.g., shouting out obscenities, profanities, and/or words that are socially taboo); these are uttered involuntarily, not deliberately or maliciously.

Warning to Parents

There are many possible causes for behaviors that could be mistaken as symptoms of a disability or disorder but are really something else. For example, when children are distractible and unable to concentrate, the teacher may assume that this behavior indicates the child has ADD or ADHD. However, there are many other possible causes of inattentive, distractible behavior, such as seizure disorder, side effects of different medications (e.g., asthma and antiseizure medications), illness of some type, lack of sleep (and possible sleep disorders), posttraumatic stress disorder, and situations at home that are causing the child stress (e.g., divorce and custody battles, chaotic home life with inappropriate expectations placed on the child). We need to be careful in our assumptions. Any diagnosis of a disorder is complex and needs to involve gathering of information and data from professionals qualified to obtain and interpret the data, as well as ruling out of other possible causes of symptoms. If you are dissatisfied with a diagnosis, follow your intuition and seek other professional assistance. Parents of children with disabilities often need to go through a maze of doctors and specialists until they feel they are on the right path of help for their child. See the section "Valuable Resources for Parents," which includes information on national organizations that offer a wealth of information on a range of disabilities.

Specific Learning Disabilities

Of all the categories of disabilities, learning disabilities (LD) are the most common and prevalent, with the highest number of children identified as LD and receiving special education. Learning disabilities can cause difficulty with language, memory, listening, conceptualization, speaking, reading, writing, spelling, math, and motor skills, in various combinations and degrees. Learning disabilities are a neurological handicap and set of conditions that interfere with the ability to store, process, or produce information, and they affect between 5 and 15 percent of the population. Each individual is unique in the combination of strengths and weaknesses and degree of impairment. Learning disabilities can be mild and subtle and may go undetected; or they may be severe, greatly affecting the ability to learn academic, communication, functional, and social skills. Learning disabilities may affect any combination of the reception or input of information into the brain (visual and/or auditory perception), the integration of information in the brain (processing, sequencing, organization), the retrieval of information from storage (auditory and/or visual memory), and the output or expression of information (communicating through motor skills or through oral/written language).

Learning disabilities create a gap between a person's true capacity and his or her day-to-day performance and functioning in various ways. The current criteria for classification as learning disabled require that the child has at least average intelligence yet is underachieving to his or her measured potential in one or more academic areas (e.g., reading, math, written language). This significant discrepancy between measured ability and performance is not due to mental retardation, emotional disturbance, environmental deprivation, or sensory impairment (vision or hearing problems).

In the past, children with learning disabilities were frequently mislabeled as having limited capacity to learn or being lazy. Over the past three decades or so, education and awareness have increased regarding specific learning disabilities. It is recognized that children with LD are not lazy or unmotivated; they have many strengths along with their areas of weaknesses. Many individuals with LD are gifted intellectually and/or have exceptional aptitude in some areas (e.g., musically, artistically, athletically). Children who are evaluated and meet eligibility criteria under IDEA (with learning disabilities that significantly affect their learning and achievement) are eligible for a range of special education programs and services. Most children with LD who qualify for special education and receive services do so because of reading and language disabilities.

Learning disabilities are considered "hidden handicaps" because they aren't visible or apparent to others in most cases—at least on the surface. Children with LD appear normal and capable.

This can make it difficult for others to understand why it can be such a struggle for children with LD to learn.

Generally children are not identified or diagnosed with learning disabilities until they are in school. However, you may begin to suspect that your child does have some specific learning disabilities in earlier years. Following are areas in which a person may have specific learning disabilities, as well as sample strategies and activities for coping with those disabilities. Every individual with LD has his or her own profile of strengths and weaknesses. No one has disabilities in all of the areas, just in some—and to varying degrees of severity. The best approach in teaching children with learning disabilities is to teach them through their areas and channels of strengths and to provide them with experiences that will build up those areas of weaknesses.

VISUAL PROCESSING DEFICITS

If your child is having difficulty making sense out of or interpreting and remembering information he or she sees, he or she may have deficits in the following visual processing areas. Have your child's eyes tested first to rule out any possible vision problems.

Visual Figure-Ground

This is the ability to identify/recognize a specific object or shape against a background. Children with this problem often lose their place while reading, skip lines, have difficulty locating a specific item on a printed page, and have trouble finding letters, words, and other items written on charts, lists, or the chalkboard. They typically have trouble completing work presented on crowded pages and will skip or omit sections.

It helps to present visual information with an uncluttered background. Color-highlight specific information you want the child to be able to see and focus on. Build practice through activities such as having your child locate pictures in different scenes or backgrounds (e.g., find the picture of the dog's bowl, his doghouse, the fence).

Visual Discrimination

This is the ability to differentiate likenesses and differences in objects, shapes, and other items. Visual discrimination is essential to reading, writing, and arithmetic. Children with this difficulty have a hard time matching letters, numbers, shapes, patterns, and designs. They have trouble recognizing the difference between symbols or shapes that look similar (e.g., *E/F, u/v, n/h,* circles/ovals, a button with two holes and a button with three holes, and so forth). If shown three or four pictures in a row with three being identical and one different in some way (e.g., color, size, position), the child would likely not be able to identify which one is different from the rest.

Provide experiences for your child such as matching activities, sorting, and playing games in which your child needs to find which one is the same or which one is different among three to five items or pictures. For example, given a set of four dog pictures, three would match as identical, and one of the four would look different in some way.

Spatial Relations or Position in Space

This is the ability to perceive objects in space and in relation to other objects. A child with this difficulty makes numerous reversals and inversions and has trouble differentiating between and remembering those letters, numbers, and shapes that are similar looking except for how they are positioned in space (e.g., *b/d/p/q; 6/9, u/n, mom/wow*). This difficulty affects understanding of directionality—left/right and up/down. The deficit manifests itself in all academic areas—reading, writing, and math.

Provide experiences for your child to build body awareness of directionality and spatial awareness (e.g., through Simon Says games). Examples: "Put the block *in* the box, *over* the box, *next to* the box, *under* the box." "Find the picture (in a row of four or five) that is facing in a different direction from the others" (e.g., three horses in a row are facing to the left, one horse is facing to the right; three pencils are pointing up, one pencil in a row is facing down).

Visual Closure

This is the ability to anticipate and supply missing visual elements by using context clues—recognizing a symbol or object when all of it is not visible. Children with this problem may have difficulty in visualizing a whole and omit portions or details from objects or symbols when they write or draw. The child may have trouble with dot-to-dot activities, identifying what an object is if part of the picture is missing (e.g., picture of half or two-thirds of a house or bird). The child may have difficulty with tasks like putting together puzzles and typically struggles with spelling and writing because he or she can't visualize the whole product.

Build these skills by first giving your child puzzles of a very few pieces and building up to more. As the pieces are being put together, have your child guess what it is supposed to be. Show partial pictures of recognizable objects and have your child guess what they are supposed to be. This can be done by covering part of the picture with your hand or piece of paper so only some of it is showing. Any hidden picture activities that are designed for young children are good practice if not too frustrating. Draw very simple objects with something important that is missing. Have your child try to identify the missing feature and what needs to be filled in to make it whole (such as the second wheel on the bike, the other eye on the face, the line to complete the frame of the house).

Visual Sequential Memory

This is the ability to recognize, recall, and reproduce visually presented materials in the correct order. Weakness with visual memory makes it hard to remember how to write letters or numbers without models to refer to. The child often has difficulty recognizing the same word on the page even if it appears numerous times and approaches it as a new word each time he or she sees it. Little "sight" words—those that are learned by visual recognition and not by "sounding out" (e.g., *from, of, said, was, the*)—are hard for the child to remember how to read and spell. The child may be able to remember all of the parts in a word (e.g., know the letters in his or her name) but gets them in the wrong sequence when reading and writing (e.g., frequently misspelling his or her name, writing *gril* for *girl*). The child often has difficulty recalling how to form numerals, and missequences when reading and writing numbers and performing math calculations.

Provide your child with experiences in which you make a game out of remembering what he or she sees after a brief exposure to build visual memory. Put two or three objects on the table in front of the child. Tell your child to name the objects and then close his or her eyes while you make one of them disappear. Then have your child open his or her eyes and tell you which one is missing. Play different variations of this game, building up to more objects. Simple games of Concentration—turning pictures over and trying to remember where and what they are to find the matches—is good for building visual memory. So are games in which you try to remember details of what you see. For example, look carefully together at a picture and then make a game out of trying to remember what was in the picture (e.g., lady on a bench, boy skating). (*Note:* This is also excellent for building expressive language, which is used when a child is asked to describe something with words.) Build visual sequential memory through games in which objects or pictures (first two or three, building up when your child masters this level) are put in an order, mixed up, and your child has to try putting them back in the original sequence/order. Do so with a sequence of blocks (e.g., two reds and then a yellow); after your child watches you and tries to remember what he or she sees, mix up the blocks and see if your child can put them back in the same order. Have your child try to remember and then perform sequences of hand signals or motions you make (e.g., hands on head, hands on waist, hands on knees).

Visual-Motor Integration

This is the ability to use visual cues to guide the child's physical movements. The child with this difficulty is often clumsy and uncoordinated in large muscle movements. He or she generally has trouble copying from the board or book (onto paper). It is often a struggle for this child to execute art projects, write on and within the lines, and align numbers when doing math problems. Typically, the child with this weakness demonstrates poor spacing and organization when writing.

Provide your child with as many opportunities as possible that build motor skills and eye-hand coordination. Don't push paper-and-pencil activities; instead spend time developing large and fine muscle movements through fun activities (e.g., crafts; dance; copying pattern designs to string beads; cutting and pasting; tracing letters, shapes, and numerals in/on various textures and materials such as sandpaper, shaving cream, etc.). See the section "Strategies for Building Fine Motor and Prewriting/Writing Skills" for many ideas in this area. Do anything fun that involves your child performing something physically by watching and copying (e.g., follow a leader doing movements such as "hands on head . . . hands on knees . . . hop . . . hop . . . turn around in a circle").

Visual Association

This is the ability to make sense out of or relate visual symbols in a meaningful way. Children with this problem may have difficulties interpreting pictures, reading or interpreting graphs and charts, and seeing how objects that are related go together.

Play matching games—finding objects or pictures of things that go together as a match (e.g., lock/key, stethoscope/nurse). Play classification games in which your child finds/identifies objects or pictures of objects that fall within the same category (e.g., various tools, fruits, farm animals, vehicles). Use wordless picture books and have your child tell you the story based on interpretation of the pictures. Give your child three or four pictures that represent sequential steps in a procedure or that tell the sequence of events in a story. Have your child put them in the correct order. (This is an excellent activity for improving visual sequencing as well as visual association and reasoning.)

AUDITORY PROCESSING DEFICITS

If your child is having difficulty making sense out of or interpreting and remembering information he or she hears, he or she could have deficits in the following auditory processing areas. Have your child's ears tested to rule out any possible hearing problems. *Note:* The section "Playing with Sounds and Language" contains numerous activities that can build your child's skills in all of the following auditory processing areas.

Phonological Awareness

This is the understanding that speech is composed of parts, and the smallest part is the phoneme. Phonemes are the distinct individual sounds that are put together to form the words we speak. See the section "What Is Phonemic and Phonological Awareness?" which provides important information about phonemic and phonological awareness—the understanding that spoken words are made up of a sequence of sounds, which is a fundamental prerequisite to learning how to read and write.

Auditory Reception

This is the ability to understand the spoken word. Any experience you give your child in which he or she will be listening to language and learning new vocabulary words builds auditory reception. Telling stories, reading books, singing songs, talking about experiences and happenings in the child's life, looking through picture dictionaries and various books in which objects and their names are pointed out are all examples.

Auditory Discrimination

This is the ability to distinguish one sound from another. Being able to do so is critical to reading and spelling success, as well as to acquiring, understanding, and using spoken language. Children with problems in this skill cannot tell when some sounds or words that sound similar are the same or different (e.g., *pin/pen, fan/van, bus/ buzz*). If you ask your child to listen as you say pairs of sounds or pairs of words and tell you if they are the same or different, that is a measure of auditory discrimination (e.g., */m/m/ /b/d/, net/net, wig/wag, mad/mat*).

Have your child listen to sounds in the environment (e.g., car honking, tea kettle whistling, dog barking) and identify those sounds. Play listening games in which your child has to listen for the word that starts with a different sound than the others (e.g., *soup, sun, mop, sand).*

Auditory Closure

This is the ability to anticipate and identify the whole when only part of the auditory information is presented. It involves tasks such as supplying missing words or word parts, as in leaving off the end of a rhyme and having the child supply the rhyme based on the rest of what he or she heard. It involves auditory blending, or being able to hear individual sounds or phonemes of a word (e.g., /m/ . . . /a/ . . . /n/) and recognizing that as the word *man.* A child with this difficulty can't easily blend sounds into syllables and words. When reading the word *fast,* the child may correctly sound the word out /f/a/s/t/ but not be able to blend the sounds together to say the whole word *fast.* If hearing the word *ham . . . bur . . . ger,* the child may not recognize that word as being *hamburger.* Practice playing these kind of listening games when words are stretched out and said slowly and the child has to say the words quickly, as a whole.

Auditory Sequential Memory

This is the ability to recognize, remember, and/or reproduce a sequence of auditorily presented/verbal data in the correct order after hearing it. Children with this weakness have great difficulty remembering and following a series of directions, remembering telephone numbers and messages, learning months of the year in sequence, memorizing multiplication tables, and so forth. A deficit in this area often affects spoken language and causes difficulty in reading and spelling because words consist of a sequence of sounds. It is typical that children with this difficulty when reading or spelling may "sound out" the word in the wrong order—all the letters/sounds may be there but out of sequence.

Build these skills by having your child repeat back to you a series of a couple/few words and phrases or simple sentences. Always make a game out of it and start with a sequence to recall and repeat that is easy and at a success level (e.g., two or three) for your child before building up to a higher level. Have your child repeat and follow directions. Play listening games in which your child tries to remember a sequence of some type. (Stories and songs that are cumulative—adding on something new with each verse—are great fun and practice.) If your child has an auditory sequential memory difficulty, he or she may have trouble learning the days of the week, counting accurately in sequence, or recalling or reciting the sequence of ABCs. It is important to start working on these activities early. Keep sessions short and always at your child's level of success. Each time, review what your child has mastered and continue moving higher and higher in the sequence once your child has mastery up to that point.

Auditory Association

This is the ability to relate spoken words in a meaningful way, to classify and categorize information heard. Children with this difficulty often have trouble with listening comprehension—making sense out of what they hear. They may have difficulty with riddles and figuring out how words heard go together in some way (e.g., birds fly . . . fish ____). Expose your child to guessing games, riddles, jokes, and many stories. Play classification and association games such as choosing a category (e.g., pets, things that fly, things that have wheels) and take turns or guide your child in thinking of and naming items that fit in that category.

Verbal Expression

This is the ability to express ideas in spoken language. Encourage growth in this area through your communication with your child. While reading a story, discuss or ask probing questions that will get your child to use language (e.g., describing what he or she sees in the picture, retelling favorite parts of the story). Play games that require your child to use descriptive language. For example, play guessing games. Have your child describe a secret object to you in detail (without naming the object) for you to guess what it is. Encourage make-believe play through use of props, dolls, puppets, dress-up. This stimulates children to make up scripts and plays and to use verbal expression.

When You Are Concerned About Your Child's Development

As parents, we learn from experience. With their first child, most parents aren't sure what are normal, average, or expected behaviors, skills, and achievements. Through parenting and interacting with other parents and observing a number of children of similar ages, parents begin to see their child in relation to other children. In doing so, parents are generally relieved and/or delighted to observe that their child is developing normally (or appears advanced) compared with other children of that age.

Sometimes, however, parents will notice that their child appears to be delayed in some way—their child is not as skilled in certain areas as other children that age seem to be. When this is the case, it is best not to panic or get stressed. Realize that children grow and develop at different rates. If your child is somewhat slower than others in certain areas at this time, it doesn't mean that he or she won't catch up developmentally. Children develop unevenly—they are faster in some areas, slower in others.

It is a good idea to share any of your concerns with your child's pediatrician. Share your observations regarding how your child is functioning or performing in developmental areas, and ask the doctor if there is any cause for concern. Ask your doctor if your child is in norm with what are considered appropriate developmental milestones for your child's age.

Read the section "Developmental Milestones of 3- to 5-Year-Olds." If your child is four years old and approaching the time to enroll in kindergarten, read the sections "What Are General Kindergarten Readiness Skills?" and "Enrolling Your Child in Kindergarten or Waiting Another Year." If you are concerned about your child's development and/or readiness skills, speak with your child's preschool or kindergarten teacher and day-care providers for their observations and input.

In general, there are certain red flags that may indicate developmental delays or immaturities in different areas (e.g., language, social/emotional, cognitive, motor, academic readiness). If you notice some of the following, be sure to share your concerns with the appropriate professionals. Early intervention can make a big difference with children and lead to a better prognosis and outcome. There are many strategies that can be employed to foster growth and development in each of the areas. The sooner you can get started learning and using these strategies at home with your child and obtaining the services of specialists (if needed), the better. Watch for the following, which may indicate physical problems such as vision or hearing; language, motor, social/emotional, and cognitive delays; or immature adaptive skills:

- Fearful of new situations and people
- Excessively timid and avoids interaction with others
- Socially withdrawn or aloof
- Not interested in playing with other children or has great difficulty doing so
- Unable to focus on task for more than a couple of minutes
- Fatigues quickly, lethargic
- Trouble eating, sleeping
- Trouble learning self-care skills (toileting, washing/drying hands, dressing)
- Awkward or clumsy in motor skills and balance
- Difficulty running, jumping, hopping, climbing, throwing/catching a ball, riding a tricycle

- Difficulty holding and using a crayon, large pencil, scissors
- Difficulty with tasks such as picking up objects with fingers, stringing beads, buttoning buttons
- Very poor self-control when angry or frustrated
- Argumentative and uncooperative
- Aggressive
- Moody
- Turns head toward source of sound
- Holds things very close to face, squints eyes
- Doesn't participate or engage in many different activities
- Doesn't show excitement, curiosity, or enthusiasm
- Doesn't seem to understand or follow one- or two-step directions (e.g, "Pick up the block and bring it here.")
- Shows no interest in books and stories
- Doesn't communicate well in oral language (e.g., uses incomplete sentences; difficulty finding words to express self; others besides immediate family members find it hard to understand when child speaks; doesn't engage in conversations)
- Doesn't classify or seem to understand basic categories or things that go together (e.g., shirt, pants, socks are clothes; dog, rabbit, zebra are animals; red, green, yellow, blue are colors)

WHAT TO DO?

If your child has a disability or developmental delay, help is available. Your physician will refer you to resources and agencies in your community. Children with disabilities or developmental delays (those who demonstrate a significant difference between the expected level of development for their age and their current functioning, according to qualified personnel who are recognized by or are part of a multidisciplinary team), are eligible for special education programs from infancy. Other infants and toddlers who are eligible for special education intervention are those whom qualified personnel (recognized by or part of a multidisciplinary team) indicate have established risk conditions of known cause or are considered to be at high risk (e.g., have a combination of biomedical factors) for developmental delays and disabilities.

States are mandated to use a child-find process to identify eligible children in the early childhood years and provide those children with early intervention through coordinated interagency efforts and services. If you are concerned about your child (infant, toddler, preschooler) having a developmental delay, your health-care providers and/or school district should be able to provide the information you need to secure early childhood special education programs and service. You may also want to contact your county's early intervention office.

Under the Individuals with Disabilities Education Act (IDEA), eligible children with disabilities are entitled to a full range of special education programs and services at no cost to the parent. This includes obtaining the necessary assessments/evaluation and providing the cost of programs/services to which the child is found eligible. The law specifies that parents must be included as members of the team that makes the recommendations and decisions about how best to serve the needs of the child. Parents have the final say and must give their consent before any diagnostic procedure is initiated or any programs or services are put into effect. Parents also have the right to withdraw their child from any programs/services at any time.

Once children are referred for evaluation to determine eligibility, a multidisciplinary team of specialists is involved in the assessment. More than one specialist is always involved in making the determination. Typically, parents are interviewed to share their observations and concerns and provide information that is important in the diagnostic process. Health and developmental information is obtained to determine a child's levels of physical development (including vision, hearing, and health status) and cognitive, communication, social/emotional, and adaptive development. Observations will be made of your child (e.g., in the preschool or child-care setting) by an early childhood specialist. After review of this information, appropriate assessment personnel and case managers are assigned to do further assessment in areas of need and to develop with the parents a plan of service.

Different special education programs exist for infants and toddlers. One may involve services through home visits by specialists as needed (e.g., occupational therapist, physical therapist, teacher of the deaf and hard of hearing or visually impaired, nurse). The child's development would be monitored and parents trained in various strategies, techniques, and activities to enhance their child's development in areas of delay. Another type of program combines home visits with participation in developmentally appropriate activities within a specially designed group setting (e.g., special play group for a couple of mornings per week which are instructed or facilitated by an early childhood specialist). In other programs, specialists provide services to infants and toddlers with disabilities in regularly scheduled visits to their day-care centers and preschools. These specialists also provide information and support to caregivers, teachers, and parents.

Children with disabilities of preschool age may be found eligible for enrollment in special education classes. These programs are generally provided by and within the school district. The classes are designed with curriculum that promotes learning among children of a wide variety of ability and knowledge levels. Other designated services for which a child is determined eligible (e.g., speech/language therapy, occupational therapy, adaptive physical education) are typically provided at that school site during the school day (or half-day) preschool program. Again, contact the local school district to inquire about your concerns and your child's eligibility for these services.

Disabled children of kindergarten age are also eligible for a range of services. Often these services are provided within the regular kindergarten classroom by various specialists. Some disabled children of kindergarten age may be placed in full-day kindergarten classes designed with developmentally appropriate curriculum that provides intensive instruction, activities, and opportunities for growth in developmental areas of need (e.g., language, preacademic readiness skills, adaptive self-help). In all cases, children with disabilities, under IDEA, are to be educated in the least restrictive setting to meet the child's needs and given opportunities for maximum interaction with the general school population in a manner appropriate to the needs of the student and his or her nondisabled peers.

If your child is enrolled and attending a regular kindergarten program and you are concerned that he or she has disabilities or developmental delays, share your concerns with the kindergarten teacher and the school nurse. Appropriate specialists who serve the school (e.g., speech/language therapist, adaptive physical education teacher) should be consulted with and informed of any concerns related to their area of expertise. You may also wish to speak directly with other school personnel (e.g., principal, school psychologist, counselor, special education resource teacher or special education coordinator).

Your school may suggest scheduling a meeting with you and other members of your school's student support team (SST) to discuss the concerns; share information and input from parents, teacher, and others who have observed the child in different school settings; explore and select positive strategies and interventions to implement; and then monitor the effectiveness of the strategies and follow-up with appropriate next-step intervention. In other cases, it may be recommended to proceed with a referral for evaluation of possible special education services (e.g., speech/language evaluation). This requires parents completing paperwork and signing permission for such evaluation. After any assessment is completed, you will be invited to attend the Individualized Education Plan (IEP) meeting. At that time, team members would share the results of the assessment with you, discuss programs/services your child may qualify for, and (if eligible) develop and write an IEP with specific goals and objectives to meet the identified needs of your child.

Parents always have the right to make a referral for special education services. However, it is strongly recommended to consult with school personnel before doing so. Whenever possible, a coordinated and collaborative effort—with parents and the school team working together—is advised.

Working with Your Child's School: A Team Approach

It is well recognized that the key element of successful schools is shared responsibility or partnership in education, which involves teamwork among school personnel, parents, students, and the community. The research is clear that children do better in school when their parents play an active role in their education. Your child's preschool and elementary school needs your involvement and commitment to become part of the school community and help in whatever way you can.

Schools will generally go to great lengths to reach out to parents and solicit help and involvement—encouraging parents/grandparents to visit, volunteer in any number of capacities, attend various events and activities, join the school government or advisory committees, and so forth. Of course, not every parent has the time or desire to be a classroom volunteer on a regular basis or become an officer of the parent-teacher association. However, there are many ways to support the school program and particularly to show your interest and desire to help your child's classroom teacher and instructional program.

If you have time to volunteer in the classroom, teachers appreciate parents who can be scheduled on the calendar (e.g., once a week for an hour) to assist students in the classroom (e.g., adults who will read to/with individual or small groups of children). Parents are welcomed to work one to one or with a small group of children on some fun learning activity that the teacher has prepared. There are many organizational and clerical tasks that are of great help to classroom management and are time consuming for teachers (e.g., handling classroom libraries and check-out systems, preparing materials needed for a special project). Teachers need parent volunteers for class field trips. There are always special activities (e.g., cooking) that teachers want to do with students, but may not do because the ingredients needed for the activities may be costly and teachers generally have to pay for them out of their own money. Teachers welcome parents signing up to provide some of the ingredients/materials for special class projects. Teachers equip their rooms with various learning centers and stations, which can be time consuming to prepare and costly to stock. Teachers appreciate whatever parents can send in from home to supply those centers.

Teachers, especially in early childhood, greatly appreciate parents who know how to sew and are willing to sew or construct different projects at home. For example, teachers may need help sewing special book bags and costumes for performances or dress-up centers or different learning center activities (e.g., Alphabet Apron, ABC Pocket Book). Your teacher will be extremely grateful, for example, if you are able to make some special alphabet learning centers for the classroom. (See the book by Nancy Fetzer and Sandra Rief, *Alphabet Learning Center Activities Kit,* Paramus, NJ: The Center for Applied Research in Education, 2000, which details numerous alphabet center activities.)

It is also important to pay attention to the notices, newsletters, school marquees, and numerous forms of communication the school uses to inform you of school events and activities. Join the parent-teacher association. Attend whatever school functions you can—especially parent/teacher conferences, early childhood parenting classes or workshops, and activities your child's class is involved in. Be a visible and participating member of the school community.

You show that you support your child's learning when you prioritize the homework your child's teacher assigns. In kindergarten, this generally involves reading aloud to your child (and specific related tasks such as questioning and talking about the story), some fun learning games you can do together, and brief skill reinforcement exercises. Typically, teachers will send home newsletters or other communication letting you know what theme is being studied (e.g., plants, insects, weather, dinosaurs), a "letter of the week" that is featured, and so forth. To reinforce children's learning and the home/school partnership, teachers will ask parents to help their child find things to bring in for sharing related to the themes or topics being studied. They will ask parents to help their child locate pictures from magazines, objects from around the house, etc., that have the same beginning sound as the letter of the week being studied. Those children who do bring from home things to share with the class feel good about themselves as contributors to the lesson.

Teachers need and value any information and insights you can share about your child. No one knows your child better than you. Share with the teacher your child's interests, likes/dislikes, home situation, and any concerns you may have. If you have any worries, questions, or concerns, talk with the teacher.

If your child is experiencing a problem (e.g., learning, behavioral, social), meet with the teacher. Ask the teacher what you can do to help your child and talk about any interventions, supports, or strategies that might be provided at school to help with the problem. Monitor and follow up with whatever strategies/interventions you decide as a team to try. Ask the teacher to keep you posted about progress and/or resolution of the problem.

The Team Approach for Children with Disabilities

If your child has a disability that negatively impacts learning and performance at school, success is dependent on a team effort in the following areas:

THE DIAGNOSTIC PROCESS

When evaluating children to determine whether they have a disability and may qualify for any special education or related services, it is necessary to involve a team. Various specialists in what is called a multidisciplinary team are involved in gathering information, testing, observing, interpreting the results of any assessment, determining the existence and extent of any disabilities, and whether or not the child meets eligibility criteria for special education programs, and, if so, developing and writing the Individualized Education Plan (IEP) for the child. Parents are members of this multidisciplinary team. Parents' input is critical and will be required in the diagnostic process. Parents will be interviewed and questioned about the child's medical history (prenatal through current), developmental history, and relevant family history and background.

THE TREATMENT OR INTERVENTION PLAN

If a child qualifies for special education or related services, a variety of school personnel and resources are likely to be involved in the provision of services (e.g., classroom teacher, special education teacher, speech/language therapist, instructional aide). Children with disabilities and special needs often have intervention outside of school involving medical and mental health professionals, various services, and therapy. It is important and in the child's best interest to have a collaborative relationship with open communication between the different professionals involved in treating the child at home, at school, and in the community. Parental consent in writing is required for school personnel, doctors, and other care providers outside of school to share information and strategies. If a child is receiving medication as part of treatment, close monitoring and communication among the school, home, and doctor is required (especially at trial stages when proper medication and dosage are being determined).

The IEP describes a practical plan for instruction and delivery of services to a child found eligible for special education. It includes a description of the child's present levels of educational performance (e.g., academic, nonacademic, perceptual functioning), and how the identified disability affects the child's involvement and progress in the general education curriculum and activities. The IEP specifies the special education and related services the child is eligible to receive (including the time, frequency, location/setting of instructional setting, and anticipated duration of services). When the IEP is developed, the team writes measurable annual goals for the student, and short-term objectives/benchmarks to determine progress towards meeting the goals.

Once a child is enrolled in a special education program, the teamwork and communication must continue. An IEP team meeting (including parents, classroom teacher, specialists/service providers, etc.) is held annually. At that time the team reviews the IEP to determine the child's level of growth and progress toward goals and objectives. A new IEP is written with specific goals, objectives, and so forth that address current areas of need. Ongoing monitoring and updating of intervention plans—whether they are special education plans and programs *or* more informal ones involving general education only and not special education—are important when a child is struggling in school.

Typically, children who exhibit significant behavioral challenges in the classroom will need more intensive monitoring and positive reinforcement of appropriate behaviors. Teachers will need to work closely with parents, communicating frequently about the child's progress.

PART 7

What the Experts Say

For this final part of the book, I interviewed a number of well-respected preschool teachers, kindergarten teachers, and preschool directors. They graciously shared their valuable insights and recommendations which parents should find helpful. Their advice and thoughts are based upon their expertise and awareness acquired from their many years of experience working as early childhood educators. You'll find advice on reading, playing, establishing routines, after-school activities, homework, television and computer use, going places and doing things together as a family, and more.

Advice for Parents from Interviews with Preschool and Kindergarten Teachers and Directors

I interviewed nine educators from the San Diego area (one teaching in a public school in the Los Angeles area). These experts include one preschool director and eight preschool and kindergarten teachers from private schools as well as public elementary schools. Their schools and the student populations they are working with are diverse and represent a wide socioeconomic range (schools in poor as well as affluent neighborhoods). I am grateful for their willingness to share their insights (based upon vast experience and knowledge of early childhood education). The following are excerpts from my interviews with these wonderful educators: Levana Estline, Marcia Giafaglione, Betsy Arnold, Julia Croom, Judy Medoff, Yael Estline, Christina Evans, Rachell Clavell, and Sue Sward.

School Readiness

"At the beginning of the year when I do my parent orientation, I want parents to understand that some kids come in already starting to read. Others come in not knowing any letters or sounds. Some already know how to write their names and letters. Others are not ready developmentally for that, but it's okay. They need to understand that they all develop in different ways. I try to let parents know what the expectations are going to be by the end of kindergarten—

the minimum standards we should see. Obviously, some kids will be beyond that, and maybe a couple of children won't have achieved that yet; but overall, this is what we would expect at the end of the year."

"We have some children who really need an extra year of pre-school. It's very hard for the parents. If kids are pushed too hard, they can't cope—and fall apart. It's so much better for them to have the extra year if they need it. As far as kindergarten readiness, the main thing is the social and emotional development."

"They will need to be able to follow directions, take turns, share, and be responsible for their belongings. It is important to teach young children that somebody is not always going to be able to help them pick up their things. Also, the child needs to know that in school if you need a pencil or crayon, you can't just sit there, you need to be able to ask for it."

"They will need to be able to attend to and finish a task—stay on something for a prescribed amount of time—not just starting something and saying, 'It's too hard and I don't want to do this right now.' "

"They need to know how to follow rules—and rules at school might be different than rules at home."

"To me it isn't necessary for children to enter kindergarten knowing all of their ABCs—that's the job of kindergarten. I want to see parents reading with their kids, playing with them . . . helping build their fine motor skills [by] giving them manipulatives to play with. And very important, if the child hasn't been to preschool, he/she needs experiences in learning how to cooperate and share."

"I see a lot of parents too worried about their child not knowing how to read. They feel it's their fault if their child doesn't read yet. I have to tell my kindergarten parents not to worry—it's just kindergarten. Let them develop. They will end up reading. The more you push, the harder it is on children . . . they lose self-confidence and feel like failures."

"What matters most to me for kindergarten readiness isn't how much they already know academically. That's the purpose of kindergarten—to learn all that. . . . It's more important to come to school knowing how to share and how to listen."

"Everybody is so into the academics. You get a bunch of kids who may come to school close to reading, but they can't bounce or catch a ball. It's important to do those kinds of activities. Play ball, jump, climb. Play games like walking on the cracks or lines of the sidewalk for balance and management."

"I would like kids to enter kindergarten knowing how to work cooperatively with other children in a learning kind of environment—to be able to work both in a large and small group, as well as independently. If they had been to preschool they have group experience, but now they're with twenty kids."

"It would be nice if kids who entered kindergarten understood the concept of school. When we grew up, there were lots of kids around in the neighborhood. We were out playing and mixing with all these kids; and going to school with a bunch of kids was nothing new. Most of my students are sheltered into confined populations— either just the home, or a neighbor's house, or day care. They are in controlled situations. They don't go out in the neighborhoods to play. So they aren't entering school with the awareness that when there's a whole bunch of children, things are different. With twenty students, I can't take care of each child's individual needs at exactly the time they may want me to take care of them."

"It would help if children came to school recognizing some numerals and letters. When going shopping together, prices are good numbers to read. There are numbers to read on gas station signs. Children can look for and find numerals, words, and letters all around the environment. If parents don't mind magazines or papers being color highlighted, it's a great activity to have children hunt for words (e.g., *the*) or those beginning with certain letters, and color highlighting the ones they find."

"Most of my kindergartners by the end of the year can read the CVC (three-letter consonant-vowel-consonant words such as bat, cat and sat) and at least twenty-five high frequency words. Most are writing a couple of sentences. A few of my strongest kids might be writing five- or six-word sentences, but still using a lot of in-vented or what I call 'best guess spelling'—not every word spelled correctly."

"A lot of times parents ask, 'How can I teach my child to read?' I tell parents that I can do that part. That's my job. If they would read to their child and do things like take their child to the zoo, the beach, the museum—talking about what they see . . . it is the most valuable. Then the child will have the background information they need to become good readers and students."

"One of the very best things a parent can do is read to their child. It doesn't matter what language they read to them . . . just as long as they point out words and things and discuss what's being read—in whatever language the parent is fluent in. Libraries do have books in other languages."

"The children in my class who do well are the ones who have life experiences. They've been to the zoo, to the beach . . . and then they have gone to the library afterward and checked out books that are related. They are the ones who have parents who expect them to do well, and pass on a positive attitude about school and the impor-tance of what they are learning in class. They are the ones whose parents know what's going on in school, encourage and praise their child ('You're doing great!'), and extend their school learning . . . like bringing to class a book or something to share related to what we've been studying."

"It's a very different world than it used to be. It always disturbs me, the assumption that affluent families know how to parent. We have kids coming to preschool who don't know their last names—kinds of things you wouldn't expect to find. We see parents not spending the time to communicate with their children, so kids aren't coming in with the language and communication skills that they need . . . the things they would get by taking a walk together, going to the beach, taking a look at nature . . . and *talking*. We have fami-lies with both parents who are lawyers or doctors, or some parents who are just very involved in the community or whatever, and no-body's talking to the kids."

"It is important to teach children some common courtesies and manners—like not to intrude, to say 'please' and 'thank you.' A lot of children don't seem to have been taught those kinds of things."

"It would be helpful if the teacher wasn't the first one to have to say 'no' to a child."

"The biggest change I notice from even ten years ago is that kids are so indulged behaviorally that it makes school adjustment a real problem for themselves, as well as their parents. The first thing I would like to see parents do is be consistent in what they ask of their child behaviorally. A lot of children I'm seeing today seem to know that if they insist, whine, fuss, kick, scream, yell, etc., that eventually the adult will give in, and they will get whatever it is that they want. Parents need to remember that they're the ones [who] are supposed to be in charge . . . not the child. I see kids with a lot of emotional issues based on some behavioral things that could very easily have been taken care of already. This is two- [or] three-year-old behavior that we see in five-year-old kids. In many instances it is parenting that is very inconsistent . . . parents who are trying desperately to be their child's friend, and not being their parent."

Encouraging Learning

"Children learn best when they can draw upon their strengths and interests. I had a student, Jason, who knew everything there was to know about bugs; it was a family interest. The family had a butterfly garden in their backyard. He was like an encyclopedia—knowing everything there was to know about insects. Finding their interest and doing things together as a family that reinforces that interest is so valuable. Then they come to school with so much confidence in themselves."

"The toys and games I think are best are any that promote some type of problem solving and thinking . . . also Lego and other manipulatives that build fine motor. It's important to balance out with some large motor activities, too. Swimming is great, ball play . . . anything to get eye-hand coordination involved."

"My advice to parents is help their child follow through with tasks. Direct them toward a task, but don't do it for them. Let them be independent. I have a lot of parents drop their child off in the morning and put their things away for them. Children need to develop that responsibility. Parents should encourage them to put their own belongings away—not do it for them."

"Grab the teachable moments whether they're life experiences or whether they are academic. When something comes up, put the laundry down—take a moment to spend time discussing whatever it is with your child."

"Parents don't often realize how much their kids can learn by just talking or thinking out loud. For example, at a supermarket you can say, 'Let's see, I'm figuring out how much corn on the cob to buy. That's one each, and there are four of us. But I think Daddy might eat two . . . so we need four and one more. How much is that altogether?' Or while baking cookies together say, 'I need two and a half cups. Let's fill a half of a cup. I wonder how many of these I need. Oh, did you notice two of these made one full cup?' Children need to see these concepts applied in their real life."

"Encourage your child to ask questions. Don't you do all the questioning or explaining. Ponder and get kids curious (e.g., 'I wonder why . . . the sky is blue'). Leave some questions unanswered. Keep their curiosity going and growing, and the desire to keep learning new things."

"I find that sometimes parents compare children to either siblings or other children. Parents need to let every child know he/she has strengths. It's important to teach them that they are capable and responsible little individuals. Just because they may not be as far along as other children, that's not a bad thing. It's okay because developmentally they all grow at different rates."

"It disturbs me when I see parents getting angry at their child for having a hard time learning a concept. That's the worst way to respond to a child who is having difficulty. If the parent is frustrated, imagine how frustrating it is for the child. It is important for parents to give their child encouragement. If the child doesn't get it after being shown or taught something one way a few times, there must be a different way we should be teaching it—using a different angle or approach. We have to remember that children learn in different ways. Also, they might not be developmentally ready to pick up some kind of a concept . . . and it's better then to leave it alone if something isn't really working."

"We're finding that kids—even from affluent homes—don't know what a lot of words mean that you would assume they would in kindergarten . . . words like *goose, turkey, apron, hammer* . . . simple objects that they should be able to recognize and know the names of, but they don't. That means the child needs adults talking to them—giving them experiences and along with those experiences a lot of vocabulary and language should be used . . . labeling with words and names. For example, I see a lot of people at the zoo with their kids, but not having much conversation with them about the animals. Just dragging a child through the zoo without talking about what they see doesn't fulfill a function."

"Parents are their child's first teacher, and they need to set the stage for learning. Self-esteem builds a good foundation for beginning school. If kids feel good about themselves they'll be more successful in school."

"If you're a confident little kid, you are going to know that failure is not the end of the world. If you don't remember which way *b* goes or *d* goes, you're still okay in school. Children need to have experienced a lot of successes so they can say to themselves, 'I've tried a bunch of things in life, and this is another new thing, but I can do it.' It helps when parents give encouragement and messages like, 'Remember when you were learning to ride your bike, and you fell off at the beginning? But that's okay; you know how to ride your bike now.'"

"I find that kids seem to be losing their imaginations. They need so much prompting to figure out what to do . . . even when playing dress-up . . . or thinking of something creative to do with blocks. . . . I think they're more used to things like the computer where it's click, click, click. Computers are great in many ways. They certainly are patient little tutors. They aren't going to get frustrated if you're trying to practice a new skill. But these little people need to learn to talk with people, to tell stories, to draw and color."

"I like to see my kids playing more with games—even the old favorites (e.g., Chutes and Ladders™, Candyland™, and all the different strategy games) . . . and using their imagination—even taking the cushions off the couch and pretending . . . this is the lake, and here is the . . . It seems to me that with the toys they are making now you don't have to have any imagination to play with them. They kind of do everything by themselves. For example, I have children bringing a toy to school on their 'sharing day' and I ask them to share with the group, 'Tell us about this.' The child will say that the toy does this, this, and this . . . But when I ask what do *they* have to do to play with the toy, they don't have to do anything."

"We're finding parents sometimes not willing to make the personal sacrifices to help their kids achieve in school. By that I mean, for example, kids need to have an early consistent bedtime. If parents have a football party that starts at 6 o'clock there's a conflict. Rather than get a sitter so they can go to the party, or go to the party with the child for an hour and a half and come home early. . . . Parents may not think twice about taking the child and staying until 9 or 10 at night, and expect the child to be able to function and perform the next morning."

Listening to Your Children . . . and Spending More Time with Them

"This little boy in our school was walking into the classroom. Just before the classroom he saw a bumblebee and said, 'Daddy, look at the bee.' His father said, 'Come on . . . I don't have time. I'm late; we have to hurry up.' The boy didn't give up. 'But Daddy, look at the bee.' . . . And his father said, 'I don't have time. Let's go.' Meanwhile, he's spending so much time saying, 'I don't have time.' . . . When the child persisted, 'But Daddy, look at the bee,' the dad replied, 'I've seen bees already. Let's go!' Then the boy said, 'But Daddy, you didn't see *this* bee.' Then it hit him . . . the father stopped, went over to the child, looked at the bee, and said, 'You're right . . . that is a wonderful bee.' Then they went into the classroom. I think that's a beautiful anecdote. That child was teaching his father something important that day."

"Being able to walk around the block with one of their parents at their own pace and saying, 'Look at this butterfly, and the parent saying, 'Oh, isn't it a beautiful butterfly!' . . . just feeding back what the child is saying would be far more beneficial than running to a science class."

"Our day starts at nine, but child care opens at 7:30. Parents are dropping their children off and rushing to work. It's important to take that moment and just stop, hug goodbye, and say, 'Have a great day.' Sometimes we need to model and prompt the parents—to remind them to do these things. Again, parents are very well meaning. They love their children very much. . . . They are just so very busy."

"We see parents picking up their children who have been gone all day. They don't even give their child eye contact for that one minute to give the child a hug and ask how his or her day was, before they're already talking to their friends making plans, or on their cell phones. I just think that the children need some attention . . . even if it's a few minutes . . . that's all they need . . . because they'll be happy to go off with their friends, too."

"It's important to make some time for being together with your child and doing things together—without being rushed. And it's much better to spend that time playing a game together, physically *doing* something together and *interacting* rather than just going to the movies, or something like that."

"Having some quality time with their parents means the parents are respectful of their children and don't every two seconds interrupt their time spent with the child to do something else. If the plan is to spend Tuesday afternoon together, but then every few minutes the parent is on the phone with their friends . . . that's not quality time."

"Our kids are way too programmed. There's just too much organization at too young of an age. My husband gives the example that when he was a kid, they would get together and play ball. They made up their own rules. They learned to negotiate and learned to get along. If there was a fight, they learned to settle it. Kids aren't getting the opportunity to learn these kinds of skills."

"Most of these kids by four are in soccer. We have three- and four-year-olds going to tennis. They're starting karate at three. They are in junior theatre, dance, gymnastics, I'm not criticizing these parents. They are not bad parents, and they love their children dearly. They think they're doing their kids a favor."

"I find that kids are too programmed, and nowadays they seem to have a harder time figuring out for themselves what to do ... how to entertain themselves ... how to be creative. It's like they always need something planned. In years past, maybe the child took piano lessons or some activity. It seems they now have so *many* activities."

"I wish families would play with their kids more—get down on the floor and just play and make things fun . . . not to be so stressed or thinking they should be doing things academic."

"I suggest parents turn off the TV and the computer. Instead, spend time reading a book to the child, playing simple games or puzzles. Read picture books, go through a picture dictionary and name the objects. Spend time sitting down with your child interacting and talking. It doesn't have to be for huge chunks of time."

"Kids love to talk about and write about any trips they take, any family celebrations . . . birthdays, a wedding coming up, their baby brothers and sisters, going to worship, a ball game, and so on. Their world is centered on whatever is happening to them."

"I have a few kids that all they do is watch TV or play on the computer. If they are played with or read to, it's very minimal. I wish parents would limit that TV time and engage with their child. I know it's hard as a working parent. But if they can spend twenty quality minutes with their child . . . it's so much better than having the child sit in front of a TV or computer."

"We already have enrichment classes at our school. Then a lot of time after they've spent a full day at school and they've had enrichment classes, they are running down to swimming lessons, gym classes, music classes, dance classes . . . or something else. My feeling is that it is really not what children need. What they could use at this point of the day is one of their parents or someone paying attention to them. Somebody just giving them a little bit of their time."

"Parents mean well and have the best of intentions, but one of the things we are seeing is that they don't have a lot of time to spend with their kids and families. So one of the ways they're compensating is by taking them to lots of classes and extracurricular activities. The kids are very programmed. Almost every minute there's something structured for them to do."

"There are so many planned activities in the afternoon for children—it's too much. One or two activities is nice. But kids are in so many . . . karate, swimming, ballet. . . . After school, children need to be able to just play . . . go to the park . . . invite playmates . . . and relax."

"We have some parents in our school who buy their kids every new gadget, every new toy. Kids don't need so many 'things.' There was this girl in our class one year whose parents spent so much money purchasing a ton of books each month from our book club. I remember the child saying to me, 'Nobody ever reads these books to me.' "

"Children need to know that there is some adult willing to listen to him or her. Even when picking the child up from day care in the afternoon, talking during the car ride home and finding out what's going on. Beginning readers can read to you while you're making supper. There are a lot of missed opportunities to spend time with and talk to children."

School Connections

"Ask your child specific questions about his or her day in school . . . 'Did you paint any pictures today? What colors did you use? Did you learn any new letters today? Which one?' . . . Don't just ask, 'What did you do in school today?' "

"When children come home from school, take the time to let them talk and express themselves. Just listen to them. Don't interrogate and ask too many questions."

"When we send work home to show the parents what the child has been doing in school, we ask parents to *please* sit together with your child to go through that work. Let the child show off what he/she has been learning. The kids are proud to show what they are doing and learning in school."

"Go over what has been learned in school. Practice or reinforce what the teacher has been teaching. But don't go ahead. For learning a new skill, it is better to learn it in school with the other kids the way the teacher teaches it. I always tell my students, 'Now go teach your parents what we learned today.' . . . The kids say, 'My parents already know this.' Then I tell them, 'But they didn't learn the way *you* learned it today. When they went to school they were taught differently. So you can teach it to them our way.' "

"Parents need to read to their child every night and talk about what they're reading. They should also let kids read to them whatever they can—even if it's picture telling. They need to take their children places and point things out to them."

"It will help children if after reading a book with their child, parents close the book and ask the child about it. One technique that is recommended (assuming the parent read the book in advance) is before reading to the child say, 'This book is going to be about Jacko, the elephant. When we finish the book I want you to be able to tell me two things that Jacko did.' Then, while reading the book, point out the things he did. At the end of the reading, of course, the parent would then ask the child the question."

"Simple things aren't being done at home like responding to notes when we send them out from school. For example, we might send a note saying, 'We're doing an activity in class with teddy bears. Please send in your child's teddy bear.' Nannies are getting the notes—many of whom don't speak English. Things don't get responded to. We're the ones who are telling parents, 'Your child went potty three times today. Did you know he's ready to be toilet trained?' "

"I often find that notes from school aren't answered in a timely fashion. Many times they aren't even pulled out from the child's folder or backpack. Parents need to get in the habit of checking for school communication, homework, and so forth every day."

"I think parents should make every possible effort to make a connection between home and school—to get to know the teacher and to make the child aware of the fact that they are in some sort of partnership . . . that they both care and there's some kind of accountability on both ends."

"The more parenting classes we offer (morning, afternoon, evening), our parents can't seem to get enough. Parents need support systems and they're not out there. Parents are hungry for connections. I think they're longing to feel connected. You have no idea how dependent parents are on us here; and it's increasing—the amount of dependence."

"I let parents know ahead of time what topic we're going to be studying and encourage them to send things to school for 'sharing' related to that topic. So if we're studying insects, the child might bring in an insect book from home."

Homework

"I changed my homework this past year. I use a lot of 'homework bags' (e.g., math ones, alphabet ones, fine motor ones) designed to be interactive with parents . . . not just to read a book, but which also involves doing a special activity. They require parent involvement. In the past, we would send home weekly homework that always involved about twenty minutes of reading, some brief reading activity, and usually some brief math activity to do. For parents who would think that's not enough and wanted more challenge for their child, I would have a box of stuff—extra activities—that they could look through and choose from to help their child reach their potential."

"The kind of homework I like to give are my 'homeowork bags' I make up and send home. For example, the 'Adventure Bag.' It has our mascot stuffed dog, Sparky, in it. When one of the children has that bag at home for a few days, there are directions inside with certain activities and things to do together. For example, keeping a journal about the child's adventures with Sparky. Those kids who bring the bag home early in the year have their parents record what they dictate ('Sparky and I went to soccer practice. We played on the swings. Then we went to Burger King. . . . My mom read a Clifford book to me and Sparky. Sparky fell in the bathtub.'). Those children who have that bag toward the end of the year are usually writing all of their own journal entries. I have lots of different bags such as the 'Left-Right' bag. It's filled with a few read-aloud books on left-right and directions for parents such as: 'Play "Simon Says" with your child.' 'Tie a piece of yarn around his/her right wrist.' Give directions like, 'Crinkle a piece of paper in your left hand.' "

"My homework changed last year because we went to a full-day kindergarten program. Prior to this year I always sent home a weekly packet that had some reading activity, math activity, handwriting . . . things that would reinforce what we were doing in the classroom weekly. It would take probably about ten to fifteen minutes to complete—depending on the child. When we went to a full day, I felt that after being in school so many hours, the children didn't really need a lot more to do at home. Instead, they needed some 'down' time. I told parents that the homework would be to read to their children every night. There is a calendar that is kept monthly to record that they have done the reading; and the children have a weekly oral report. The kids are assigned a day during the week for their presentation to do in front of the class. It's not long—but something they have to get up and explain; and there's a product of some type to share. At the beginning of the year, I gave them ideas to get started with for oral reports. We study colors the first week of school. If the color was red, they might do the report on something red. For example, I had one child who made red Jell-O™ and explained how he made it. Another cut out pictures of things that were red from a magazine, mounted the pictures, and talked about them."

"For homework I always give some kind of review of what was learned in class. The child should be pretty independent with any exercise sent home. It is not something the parent has to help the child with. Of course, this is in addition to asking parents to read with their child and do other basic things."

Other Observations and Advice

"I really believe the process is more important than the product. I can't give enough of fingerpainting, play dough, blocks, water tables . . . the basic, old-fashioned things."

"Another thing kids need to be able to do and often have a hard time with is sequencing simple stories. For example, 'What happened first? in the middle? last?' "

"I find kids don't know a lot of songs or nursery rhymes."

"Kids are more sophisticated nowadays—more exposed, there is so much available to them that they are exposed to. They may be more sophisticated and aware, but they're still just five."

"In any second language home, it is important to keep the second language going. There is absolutely no reason for a child to lose his or her first language, and no reason not to learn a second language. The ones who benefit the most and have the biggest advantage are those who are bilingual. I encourage bilingual parents to speak the home language with the child at certain times of the day consistently (e.g., at the dinner table) . . . so that it is always expected to speak and discuss things in that language at that time. Both languages are then reinforced."

"With the self-help skills: I have to constantly say to parents, 'With toileting needs, kids must be able to get out of their clothing.' And with some of these clothes—the snaps and buttons are so hard. Lunchboxes are another thing. Children can't open their lunchboxes. Parents generally don't realize that their kids can't even open up the Tupperware™ in their lunches or their lunchboxes; and those kinds of little things are important."

"I have parents who are very reluctant to get involved in the school. In their culture they have a lot of respect for teachers and may not feel comfortable questioning teachers. It is important that parents are aware of the fact that they are part of a team, and their voice needs to be heard. They can and should jump in if they see something is not working for their child. They need to let the teacher know if they agree with something and when they don't agree with something."

"It's very hard for parents today. It's the expectation to have a career. If you don't have a career, then you're expected to be the super volunteers. Some of them have work and then are also the super volunteers."

"I can see some of the mistakes that parents are making. I can also look back now (as a mother of grown children) with the awareness that I made a million mistakes myself."

"Parents need to follow through on discipline and consequences. Whatever that is, it needs to be consistent."

"Every adult is entitled to make his or her own decisions, but they need to think very carefully about how the decisions they make impact their child. They need to remember that they are always their child's role model. 'Do as I say and not as I do' is something that children don't respond to very well. If parents expect a certain behavior from their child, they need to model that behavior in some way, and to be really consistent. If they can't actually fulfill what they say they are going to do, their word becomes meaningless."

"Promises are another thing. If you say you're going to do something—like pick up a child at a certain time—and you break that continuously, it's hard to repair that trust. When that door opens at the end of the school day for dismissal, the kids want to see their parent. They have no concept of time. Being ten minutes late feels forever to them . . . and that's hard for children."

Additional Resources by the Author

Sandra Rief produced a video through Educational Resource Specialists (1-800-682-3528) entitled *How to Help Your Child Succeed in School—Strategies & Guidance for Parents of Children with ADHD and/or Learning Disabilities.* This video demonstrates numerous strategies and techniques across the age levels that are highly effective with all children, even though the video is targeted for children with learning difficulties (available both in English and in Spanish). It includes the following sections:

- Introduction
    - —What Does It Mean to Have Learning Disabilities?
    - —What Does It Mean to Have ADHD?
- Building Organization and Study Skills
    - —Organizing Materials and Workspace
    - —Getting through the Homework
    - —Homework Survival Kit
    - —A Few More Tips
- How Can I Help My Child with Math?
    - —Computation Strategies
    - —Learning Multiplication Tables
    - —Functional Math (Time and Money)
    - —Survival Math
    - —Games for Building Math Concepts

- How Can I Help My Child with Reading?
  - —Shared Reading and Partner Reading Techniques
  - —Questioning Strategies
  - —Books on Tape
  - —Building Word Recognition
  - —Motivate Your Child to Read
  - —Strategies to Help Focus on the Text
  - —Reading Comprehension Strategies
- How Can I Help My Child with Writing?
  - —Help to Organize Thoughts and Choose Topic
  - —Getting Them Started
  - —Help with Editing
  - —Help with Spelling
  - —Help with Fine Motor Skills
  - —Interventions to Bypass Writing Disabilities
  - —Motivate Your Child to Write
- How to Support Your Child and Avoid Damaging Relationships

Sandra is also the author of the following books:

How to Reach and Teach ADD/ADHD Children. West Nyack, NY: The Center for Applied Research in Education, 1993. (Spanish version available)

How to Reach and Teach All Students in the Inclusive Classroom (co-authored with Julie Heimburge). West Nyack, NY: The Center for Applied Research in Education, 1996.

The ADD/ADHD Checklist: An Easy Reference for Parents & Teachers. Paramus, NJ: Prentice Hall, 1997.

Alphabet Learning Center Activities Kit (co-authored with Nancy Fetzer). Paramus, NJ: The Center for Applied Research in Education, 2000.

For more information or to contact her, see the web site: **www.sandrarief.com** or call 800-682-3528.

INDEX

A

Academic skills. *See also specific skills*
  kindergarten readiness and, 13–14
Action songs, favorite, 52
Active listening, 71
Activities
  organized, 223
  physical, importance of, 47–48, 86
Adaptive skills, kindergarten readiness
  and, 14–15
Age. *See also specific ages*
  kindergarten readiness and, 10
  special education entitlements by, 205
Alphabet. *See also* Letter/sound associa-
  tion skills
  helping children learn, 108–12
  knowledge/competency of, 107–8, 150
    expected by end of kindergarten,
    121
  learning to write, 166–67
Alphabet books, 54, 109
  making, 112
Alphabetic principle, 116
  emergent readers and, 120
American Academy of Pediatrics, The,
  65
American Library Association, 58
American School Directory, 65
Anxiety disorders. *See* Emotional distur-
  bances
Art, importance of, 47, 48
AskERIC, 62
Asperger's syndrome, 187–88
Association for Library Service to Chil-
  dren, 57
Asthma and Allergy Foundation of
  America, 62
Attention
  getting and keeping child's, 69–71
  gift of undivided, 27–28
Attention deficit hyperactivity disorder
  (ADHD), 184–85. *See also* Chal-
  lenging children
  Tourette's syndrome and, 190
  video on, 231–32

Attention-getting behaviors, ignoring,
  78–79
Auditory association deficit, 200
Auditory processing deficits, 197–200
Auditory closure deficit, 199
Auditory discrimination deficit, 198–99
Auditory learners, 42
Auditory reception deficit, 198
Auditory sequential memory deficit,
  199–200
Autism, 186–87
Autism-PDD Resources Network,
  62
Autism Society of America, 62

B

Babysitters, importance of, 88
Behavior
  Asperger's syndrome and, 187–88
  autism and, 187
  consequences for negative, 78–79
  fostering positive, 84
  of good readers, 130–32
  maintaining good
    at home, 85–86
    outside home, 86–87
  parents modeling, 31
  reinforcing appropriate, 76–77
  teaching appropriate, 30
Behavioral disorders, 189–90
Behavioral problems
  kindergarten readiness and, 218–19
  preventing, 84–85
    at home, 85–86
    outside home, 86–87
  redirection for, 88
Behavioral skills
  academic success and, 67
  kindergarten readiness and, 14–15
  school expectations, 72–73
    preparing children for, 73–74
Benchmarks. *See* Developmental benchmarks
Blending sounds, 100
Book-handling skills, 122–23

233

listening skills, 71
positive social skills, 74
respectful behavior, 33
vocabulary use, 141
writing, 162
Motivation, reading and, 116
Motor skills
fine *vs.* gross, 4
kindergarten readiness and, 13
visual-motor integration deficit and,
196–97
Movement. *See* Creative movement
Music
importance of, 46–47, 48
toys for, 55

N
National Alliance for the Mentally Ill, 63
National Association for the Education
of Young Children, 59
National Child Care Information Center,
65
National Head Start Association, 59
National Information Center for Chil-
dren and Youth with Disabilities,
63
National Information Center on Deaf-
ness, 64
National Institute of Child Care and
Human Development, 64
National Institute of Child Health and
Child Development, 66
National Institute of Child Health and
Human Development (NICHD),
113
National Institute on Early Childhood
Development and Education, 59
National Library Service, The, 64
National Parent Information Network,
60
National Parent Teacher Association
(PTA), 65
Needs, awareness of child's, 67
Negative consequences. *See* Conse-
quences
Nonverbal language, 95
Number sense, 170
Nursery rhymes, favorite, 52

O
Office of Special Education and Rehabil-
itative Services, 64
Onsets, 152
Oppositional defiance disorder (ODD),
189
Oral language, 95

Organizations skills, developing, 176–77
Organized activities, 223

P
Parental expectations
appropriate, 30
self-esteem and, 36
Parental pride, self-esteem and, 35
Parents. *See also* Modeling
books recommended for, 55–56
connecting with schools, 225–27
disability diagnostic process and,
210
disability treatment/intervention plan
and, 210–11
encouraging child's learning, 219–22
importance of school involvement,
207–9
literacy resources for, 57–60
preventing reading difficulties in children, 117
taking time with children, 222–25
Parents Helping Parents, 64
Partnership for Family Involvement in
Education, 65
Patterns, recognizing, 168
Perceptual development, manipulatives
for, 50–51
Perceptual skills, kindergarten readiness
and, 13
Performance standards, kindergarten
language arts, 16–17
reading, 17–19
speaking/listening, 20
writing, 19–20
math, 20–23
Pervasive developmental disorders
(PPDs), 186–88
Phonemic awareness, 99–101, 148–49
developing through games, 104–5
kindergarten curriculum, 123
reading difficulties and, 114–15
Phonics. *See also* Decoding
beginning, 148
letter/sound association skills, 150
Phonological awareness, 99–101
deficit in, 198
developing, 149–50
developing through games, 104–5
kindergarten curriculum, 123
Phonology, 148
Physical activities
creative movement, importance of,
47–48
importance of, 86
Physical disabilities, 186